Anxious and Avoidant Attachment Recovery

Overcome Your Attachment Issues and
Learn to Build a Secure, Healthy and
Long-lasting Relationship

Linda Hill

Table of Contents

Book #2: Avoidant Attachment Recovery 147

Thank You 239

BOOK # 1

Anxious Attachment Recovery

Go From Being Clingy to Confident & Secure
in Your Relationships

Introduction

There is a metaphor that I once heard and it goes something like this: a moth is attracted to a flame, and each time it circles the flame, it gets closer to it. There comes a point when the moth gets too close and singes its wings. Wounded, the moth flies off. In a way, this describes the relationships of many people.

Have you ever experienced a relationship where your partner became too clingy, or required constant reassurance? On the other hand, perhaps this describes you. When I was much younger, I felt the most important thing was for me to be in a relationship.

Unfortunately, my relationships at that time did not last long. I would meet someone who I was interested in and we would start dating. But the more attracted I felt, the more insecure I felt. I kept anticipating that they would lose interest in me.

Sure enough, that is what occurred. However, I now believe they lost interest in me because I grew increasingly insecure when I was around them. The qualities that initially caused them to become interested in me would gradually fade away as my insecurities were exposed.

Today, I understand why I did what I did back then. I also understand that this period in my life was necessary to become who I am today. At that time, my interactions in relationships were governed by my attachment style. I am referring to anxious attachment style.

According to a 1987 study at the University of Denver, approximately 20% of the population have an anxious attachment style. This means that two out of 10 people you enter a relationship with will be anxious regarding emotional intimacy. This book will explore what an anxious attachment style is, how it is formed, what triggers this attachment style, and how you can cope with it. Whether it is you or a partner that has an anxious attachment style, understanding and being informed are the keys to moving beyond it.

Chapter 1

Attachment Styles - Our Blueprint to Intimacy

As a young adult, I was insecure regarding relationships, especially when dating men. If I was sincerely interested in a man, I often feared he would lose interest in me. This fear stemmed from the belief that I was not good enough. As a result, I was very reactive. I was honed in on what I perceived were expressions of disappointment or disapproval. In those moments, I felt that I had blown it and that they were losing interest in me.

When I was in my mid-twenties, I moved to Texas from California due to a job offer I had received. I was raised in California, and this was my first time moving to a new state. I did not know anyone in Texas, so I spent most of my time alone.

Because of this, I did not feel judged or that I had to impress anyone. Instead, I spent a lot of time in self-reflection, and I started meditating. I believe this experience was my turning point and had a transformative effect on me. I developed a greater appreciation for myself

In time, I started dating again; however, this time, it felt different. I felt more relaxed and confident. I did not panic if I felt that I was being judged or disapproved of. I realized that a shift had occurred in me. No longer did I place my self-worth in the hands of others. Instead, my sense of self-worth was embraced from within. I had learned to accept myself for who I was and became comfortable in my own skin. I learned that I was good enough just being me. I did not know it then, but I had moved beyond the influence of my anxious attachment style.

What is an Attachment Style?

So, what is an attachment style? An attachment style is the kind of bond we form with others. To better understand this, it is helpful to look at an experiment that psychologist Harry Harlow did in 1930. Before going further, I need to state that I find Harlow's experiment unethical, but it provides important insight into attachment styles.

In the experiment, Harlow separated infant rhesus monkeys from their mothers. Harlow constructed two different kinds of surrogate mothers. The first surrogate was made of metal but had an artificial nipple from which the infant monkeys could get milk. The second surrogate was covered with soft and fluffy material; however, it did not provide food.

When the baby monkeys were hungry, they went to the first surrogate. However, they would go to the second one when they sought comfort. The second surrogate provided the infant monkeys with a sense of security.

These monkeys were curious and explored their surroundings. If they felt unsure, they would return to their surrogate. However, when the infants were placed in a new environment without their surrogate, they would not explore. Instead, they would rock back and forth on the floor and suck their thumb.

Harlow's experiment showed that the monkeys' need for comfort was just as important as their need for food. With the second surrogate, the infant monkeys could build trust and confidence.

In 1969, psychoanalyst John Bowlby wrote about his theory of attachments in humans. Bowlby believed that attachments were an instinctive emotional connection that promoted the exchange of care, comfort, and pleasure. From an evolutionary standpoint, Bowlby believed that attachments are necessary for our survival as a species.

We form attachments with our primary caregiver from the moment of our birth until around three years of age. The quality of the attachments that we form determines our ability to trust others and our level of self-confidence.

As with the baby monkeys, if we meet our emotional needs, we develop the confidence to explore the unfamiliar and trust others. However, when we do not get our emotional needs met, we may have challenges in being able to trust or explore the unknown. Research has identified four different styles of attachment:

- Secure attachments

- Anxious attachments

- Avoidant attachments

- Disorganized attachments

These attachment styles will be discussed in detail in a later chapter. For now, secure attachments lead to trust in others and confidence within ourselves. The remaining attachments are based on fear and are collectively known as insecure attachments. They lead to anxiousness and mistrust of others. It is for this reason that knowing your attachment style is important.

The type of attachment that we develop as young children may remain with us into adulthood, and influence our interactions within our adult relationships, especially intimate ones. The following are examples:

1. **Secure Style:** You feel secure in your own space and can be open and supportive toward your partner.

2. **Anxious Style:** You do not trust your partner's feelings for you and need continuous reassurance from them.

3. **Avoidant Style:** You have trouble opening up or showing your emotions.

4. **Disorganized Style:** You do not trust your partner or others. You either push people away or have an unhealthy need for closeness.

It is estimated that 56% of the population has the secure style, 20% exhibit the anxious style, 23% the avoidant style, and 1% the disorganized style.

The Attachment Styles

In the 1970s, Ainsworth conducted a landmark study known as the Strange Situation Study. In the study, she looked at how children between 12-18 months responded to their mother leaving them alone for brief moments and then returning.

The experiment began with the mother and child being in a room alone. Ainsworth looked to see if the child would explore the room under their mother's supervision. Afterward, a stranger would enter the room, talk to the mother, and approach the child. The mother would then leave the room but return shortly to comfort her child.

Ainsworth used her observations of the children to create the three major attachment styles: secure attachment, anxious attachment, and avoidant attachment. According to attachment theory, the memory of our connection to our primary caregivers is retained into adulthood, though we may be unconscious of it. In adulthood, we seek out partners that reflect that connection.

The attachment styles represent the quality of those connections. Take a moment to consider which of the following statements you most identify with:

1. It is easy for me to feel connected to others. I am willing to depend on those I feel close to, as I am comfortable with having them depend on me.

2. I am not satisfied with the level of closeness in my relationships. I feel others are not as close to me as I would like. I am frequently concerned that my partner does not really love me, or that they would rather not be with me.

3. I am uncomfortable getting close to others and feel uncomfortable when they try to get close to me. I have experienced situations where others wanted me to become more intimate than I am comfortable with.

These three statements characterize the three styles of attachment. The fourth attachment style, disorganized attachment, is a blend of the anxious and avoidant styles. Because of this fact, along with it being a rarity, it will not be discussed in this program. The following is a more detailed look at the three styles:

Secure Attachment Style

It is easy for me to feel connected to others. I am willing to depend on those I feel close to, as I am comfortable with having them depend on me.

You may have a secure attachment style if you identify with this statement. This attachment style leads to healthy and long-lasting relationships and is forged by having a secure relationship with one's primary caregiver. Developing a secure attachment style in a child does not require that the parent or caregiver be perfect.

No parent can be fully in tune with their child's needs 24 hours a day. These parents may misinterpret their child's nonverbal cues, but they continue trying different things until they meet their needs. Because the child knows they are supported, they can freely express their need for validation or reassurance without fearing punishment.

In Ainsworth's experiment, she found that children who had a secure attachment showed the following:

- They freely explored the room while their mother was there.

- They sought their mother's comfort when they were scared or unsure.

- When their mother returned to the room, they greeted her with positive emotions.

- They preferred being with their mother than with a stranger.

Early interactions with their primary caregiver make the child feel safe, understood, and valued. The child feels this way because their primary caregiver is emotionally available to them. Further, their primary caregiver is self-aware of their own emotions and behavior. The child learns from the primary caregiver and models their behaviors. You probably have a secure attachment style if you:

- Can regulate your emotions.

- Readily trust others.

- Can communicate effectively.

- Can ask for emotional support.

- Are comfortable being alone.

- Are comfortable in close relationships.

- Can self-reflect on your relationships.

- Connect easily with others.

- Can manage conflicts.

- Have good self-esteem.

- Are emotionally available.

As a result, those who carry their secure attachment style into adulthood are emotionally secure and can navigate relationships healthily. They are trusting, loving, and emotionally supportive toward their partners.

Anxious Attachment Style

I am not satisfied with the level of closeness in my relationships. I feel others are not as close to me as I would like. I am frequently concerned that my partner does not really love me or that they would rather not be with me.

You may have an anxious attachment style if you identify with this statement. This attachment style occurs when the child learns they cannot depend on their primary caregiver to meet their comfort needs. Insecure attachment styles result from inconsistent parenting and not being attuned to the child's needs.

The child does not feel a sense of security with their primary caregiver. Inconsistent parenting creates confusion for the child. In Ainsworth's experiment, children with an anxious attachment style exhibited high distress when the mother left the room.

Inconsistencies in parenting are not the only way anxious attachment styles can occur. The experience of traumatic events can also be a cause.

Another cause can be if parents are overprotective of a child. In this case, the child may pick up on their parents' anxiety and become fearful.

Those with an anxious attachment style may have had a primary caregiver who:

- Was inconsistent in comforting their child. Sometimes they may have coddled the child, while other times were indifferent or detached.

- Was easily overwhelmed.

- Alternated between being attentive toward the child and pushing them away.

- Made the child feel responsible for how they felt. It is believed that this kind of parenting can lead the child to become codependent later in life. They grow up believing they are responsible for other people's feelings.

Signs that you may have the anxious attachment style include:

- Being codependent

- Strong fears of rejection

- A dependency on your partner for validation or to make you feel better emotionally

- Having clingy tendencies

- Overly sensitive to criticism

- A need for validation from others

- Problems with jealousy

- You have difficulty being alone

- Low self-esteem

- Feeling unworthy of love

- A strong fear of abandonment

- Issues with trust

In relationships, the anxious attachment style can show up as the following:

- The person with this style does not feel worthy of being loved and needs continuous validation from their partner.

- They believe that they are responsible for the challenges in the relationship.

- They can be intensely jealous.

- Their low self-esteem causes them to distrust their partner.

- They may be overly sensitive to their partner's behaviors and emotions and jump to conclusions about their partner's intent.

All of these signs come from a strong fear of being abandoned. Though the person may want an intimate relationship, their fear of abandonment prevents them from developing the relationship they desire. Those with this attachment style may focus on their partner's needs while dismissing their own.

Traits of anxious attachment styles can also develop in adults. If someone experiences inconsistent behavior from their partner, they can develop traits of this style. If a partner is inconsistent in expressing affection, or if they are emotionally abusive, it can lead to the other person developing anxiety or insecurity about the relationship. An example of this is abusive relationships.

If a person is in a relationship with a partner who constantly tells them they are incompetent or unintelligent, that person may eventually believe it. This belief may cause them to cling to their partner. They will rely on their partner to care for them because they do not feel they can make it on their own.

Avoidant Attachment Style

I am uncomfortable getting close to others and get uncomfortable when they try to get close to me. I have experienced situations where others wanted me to become more intimate than I am comfortable with.

Those with an avoidant attachment style cannot form long-term relationships as they are challenged by a fear of emotional and physical intimacy. This attachment style is found in children who had primary caregivers that were strict, emotionally unavailable, or absent. As children, these individuals may have experienced:

- Not being supported and left to fend for themselves.

- They were expected to be independent before they were ready to be.

- Punished for depending on their primary caregivers.

- They were rejected by their primary caregivers when they expressed their emotions or needs.

- Their basic needs were not given high priority.

While such primary caregivers may have behaved this way due to outright neglect, others may have been overwhelmed with other responsibilities. Either way, these children grew up to be strongly independent. They are uncomfortable looking toward others to get their needs met, or for support.

You may have an avoidant attachment style if:

- You continuously avoid emotional or physical intimacy.

- You are fiercely independent.

- You avoid expressing your feelings.

- You have a dismissive attitude toward others.

- You are unable to trust others.

- You feel anxious when others try to get close to you.

- You avoid interacting with others.

- You believe that you do not need other people.

- You have commitment issues.

In relationships, those who have this attachment style keep their distance. Because they do not desire emotional intimacy, they never develop relationships where emotional depth is experienced.

The partners of those with avoidant attachment commonly feel that they do not know them and feel stone-walled when the other person feels the relationship is becoming too serious. In Ainsworth's experiment, children with the avoidant attachment style showed no preference between their mother and the stranger. Further, they did not seek out comfort from their mothers.

How Attachment Styles are formed

Attachment styles can be thought of as the lasting emotional connection between two individuals. In this relationship, each individual seeks the other for security and closeness.

In adult-child relationships, attachment is demonstrated by the adult responding to the child's needs sensitively and appropriately. Additionally, attachment by the child is formed not to the adult who spends the most time with them, but rather by the adult that meets more of the child's needs.

The meeting of the needs of the child is the essence of attachment theory. More specifically, the attachment theory centers on the need for security by the child. The child needs to be able to find security when it feels threatened or unsure.

One of the early founders of the attachment theory was psychoanalyst John Bowlby. In 1969, Bowlby published his theories on the subject. Bowlby believed that attachments were essential for the survival of our species because they were an emotional connection that caused babies to remain close to their mothers. From this emotional connection, Bowlby concluded that the following characteristics of attachment are meaningful to babies in their relationships with their caregivers or parents:

Closeness: Babies desire to stay close to those with whom they have formed attachments.

Safety: Babies look to their primary caregiver for safety when they are feeling unsure or fearful.

Comfort: By being a source of comfort, the primary caregiver creates the opportunity for babies to develop the confidence they need to explore their surrounding environment.

Separation Anxiety: Because of their dependency on their primary caregivers, babies experience fear when they are not around.

If the primary caregiver to the child is attentive to the child's needs, then the child learns to associate the primary caregiver with being a dependable source for getting their emotional needs met. They will develop what is known as a secure attachment style.

However, if the primary caregiver is not attentive to the child's needs, the child learns they cannot depend on their primary caregiver to meet their needs. The child will develop what is known as an insecure attachment style. The child's ability or inability to trust their primary caregiver to meet their needs may carry over into adulthood. When this happens, the person's childhood experience will be projected onto adult relationships.

If the child can trust their primary care giver in meeting their needs, they will more likely be able to trust their partners when they are adults. They will be able to experience emotional intimacy with them. However, if the child learns they cannot trust their primary caregiver to meet their emotional needs, they will have difficulty trusting their partners. Unless a conscious effort is made to change, they will be unable to experience emotional intimacy with their partners.

As with the baby monkeys, if we meet our emotional needs, we develop the confidence to explore the unfamiliar and trust others. However, when we do not get our emotional needs met, we may have challenges in being able to trust or explore the unknown.

The Causes for an Insecure Attachment

There are a number of factors that can lead to young children developing an insecure attachment style:

- The primary caregiver was young or inexperienced.

- The primary caregiver suffered from depression.

- The primary caregiver was addicted to drugs or alcohol.

- The primary caregiver or child experienced trauma.

- The child experienced physical neglect, such as improper nutrition, inadequate exercise, or unaddressed medical issues.

- The child experienced emotional abuse or neglect. Examples of this are the primary caregiver did not provide emotional attention to the child, did not attempt to understand the child's feelings, or was verbally abusive toward the child.

- The child experienced physical or sexual abuse.

- The child experienced separation from the primary caregiver due to divorce, adoption, illness, or death.

- The child lacked consistency in a primary caregiver figure. An example of this would be a child who experiences a succession of daycare staff or nannies.

- The child did not experience stability in placements. One example is a child who experiences constant change in their environment, such as moving from foster home to foster home.

In the early 21ˢᵗ century, the National Research Council and the Institute of Medicine's Committee on Integrating the Science of Early Childhood Development came to a conclusion that would shape its policies and practices. The conclusion was: "Children grow and thrive in the context of close and dependable relationships that provide love and nurturance, security, responsive interaction, and encouragement for exploration. Development is disrupted without at least one such relationship, and the consequences can be severe and long-lasting."

The Power of Connection

The most fundamental premise of attachment theory is that a child's fear is reduced when they are in proximity to the person with whom they have formed an attachment. What creates trust in the child is the child's perception of the availability of the person to be there to comfort them and make them feel safe.

When a child believes that their caregiver is both available and responsive to them, they can determine whether or not they can handle a perceived threat. If they feel they are capable, they will feel less anxiety and fear.

The body of research in attachment theory also shows that infants can receive complex information about the social interactions they observe. The information that is being referred to is both social and emotional in nature. In other words, infants can determine if the interactions they witness are caring or adversarial.

Studies using puppets showed that infants could identify whether the puppets' relationship was supportive and helpful or if it was hindering. The infants showed a preference for those puppets that were helpful toward others. The infants did this because they already knew how the puppets should behave from previous observations modeling cooperative behavior.

The study demonstrated that infants could determine how the adults in their world behave toward each other. The infants then responded to the adults accordingly through their emotions and behaviors.

For children to feel that they have someone who they can depend upon for security not only has an emotional and behavioral effect on them, but it also can have a physiological effect, as demonstrated in a 1970s experiment. It was discovered that there is a physiological response in infant rats separated from their mothers. When the rat pups were separated from their mother, they demonstrated multiple changes in their physiological and behavioral levels. Body temperature, heart rate, food intake, and willingness to explore were all affected.

What was interesting is that not all the rat pups responded in the same way. Those rat pups that received the most attention from their mothers (in the form of maternal licking, grooming, and optimal nursing position) were least affected by being separated from their mothers. They also explored more than the other pups. The pups' development was tracked over time, and these differences in response to maternal separation were found to be maintained into adulthood.

Attachment research conducted in 1996 revealed that toddlers with an anxious attachment style had elevated cortical levels, a stress hormone when introduced to novel stimuli. The rise in cortical levels was also seen when mothers stopped interacting emotionally with their children. These same results were found with children from violent homes, even when they were not directly exposed to the violence.

All evidence from the research points to the same thing. For healthy development, children need a caregiver that provides them with a sense of security, and they need to feel that they can depend on that security when needed.

Internal Working Model of Attachment

Inside the Mind of an Infant

From the time it is born, a child gains experiences from its interactions with its primary caregiver. It is from these experiences that a mental representation is formed. In attachment theory, these mental representations are known as internal working models of attachment

(IWM). IWMs influence how children interact and form relationships with others. The child's expectations when interacting with others and forming relationships are based on their IWM.

A child's IWM is like a GPS or internal guidance system. It lays down the path for how the child will respond emotionally and behaviorally to others. This pathway can endure throughout the child's lifetime if there is no conscious decision by the person to change to a more empowering way of interacting with others and themselves.

The challenge is that these IWMs operate beyond our conscious awareness, which is why changing them is difficult. If not consciously addressed by the person, or if there are no intervening events in the person's life, their IWM will remain operative throughout their lives. For this reason, the quality of the parent-child relationship in the early stages of life is a good predictor of the child's relationships when they become adults.

It is from these IWMs that the attachment styles are based. Those with a secure attachment style will have a positive image of themselves and others and are comfortable with closeness and intimacy. Studies show that children who have formed a secure attachment style by age one are more likely to have positive relationships with others besides their parents. They are more likely to have positive relationships with their peers and teachers as well.

Unless there is some form of intervention, IWMs can become intergenerational. Children with a secure attachment style are more likely to pass on the secure attachment style to their own kids when they become parents.

Those with an anxious attachment style will have a negative image of themselves but a positive view of others. These people will fear intimacy and have a fear of abandonment. As parents, they are more likely to be abusive and create anxious attachments in their children.

Those with an avoidant attachment style will have a positive image of themselves but a negative one of others. They will be overly independent and uncomfortable with closeness.

The Stages of Attachment Development

Bowlby has identified four stages in the development of attachments. They are pre-attachment, attachment in the making, clear-cut attachment, and goal corrected.

Pre-Attachment

The pre-attachment stage occurs between birth and two months. During this early stage, the infant shows interest and is responsive to interactions with anyone they encounter. They have a general attachment in that they have not yet developed an attachment to any single individual. For this reason, they are not stressed if a loving and responsive caregiver takes over for the primary caregiver. What is important to the infant is that the person can comfort them.

Attachment-in-the-Making

This second stage occurs between two and six months. The infant begins to develop a preference for an individual caregiver. They express their attachment through smiling and vocalizing. This is also the stage when the infant shows anxiety when they encounter someone they do not know. For the infant, this is a reaction to potential danger.

At this stage of attachment development, the baby does not only develop an attachment with its primary care giver but with others as well. This is also the stage when babies become more mobile and start to explore. They start crawling to investigate their world while keeping an eye on the primary caregiver. The presence of the primary caregiver gives the baby the confidence to explore.

Clear—Cut Attachment

Occurring between six months and two years, this is the stage where the child develops a strong attachment to their primary caregiver. They show signs of distress if separated from the primary caregiver for more than a brief period of time. In cases of prolonged separation, children can develop major trauma should they not be able to form a new attachment.

At this stage, the child's attachment with others is deeply ingrained. The child has created IWMs of its relationships. As the child ages, this internal model becomes more and more difficult to change.

As our IWMs operate subconsciously, they become our version of reality. We may not even be aware that our relationship issues are due to our attachment styles, because we have lived by our IWMs for most of our lives. If we become aware of how these models affect us, it takes a patient but determined effort to overcome their influence.

Goal-Corrected Partnership

This fourth stage occurs from age three to adolescence. This is the stage where there is greater tolerance for not having to be with the primary caregiver, given that the child knows where their caregiver is and their availability to them. It is also the stage when children learn that others are separate individuals with their own personalities, thoughts, and desires.

At this phase, there is a transformation in the child's attachment relationships. The child's understanding of relationships moves from focusing on getting its needs met to one where reciprocal relationship are formed. This is the stage where the child uses language to express their needs and is aware of space and time. At this stage, the child can benefit by regularly engaging with others, as in the case of pre-school.

How children respond in stage four will be shaped by the quality of attachments they form in the earlier stages.

What goes into a Child's Attachment?

Two factors determine how a child's attachments will develop: quality and critical period.

Quality

Research shows a child's primary attachment figure is not based on how much time a person spends with the child, but rather the quality of the time that the person provides them. The primary attachment is the strongest form of connection for the child. The child also forms additional attachments with those other than the primary attachment figures.

These additional attachments, also known as subsidiary attachments, vary in their level of intensity. A baby can form stronger attachments with people other than the primary caregiver if others provide a greater quality experience than the primary caregiver.

Critical Period

The critical period, also known as the sensitive period or the attachment in the making stage, is the period when a child's early attachments are formed. During this time, the brain's plasticity is receptive to the influence of the attachment experience. When this period passes, the child's attachment pattern becomes deeply ingrained and difficult to change.

Theories on Attachment Formation

This chapter covered the importance of forming attachments, the stages of attachment forming, and the factors that influence the creation of attachments. But how are attachments formed? There are two theories regarding this: learning theory and evolutionary.

Learning Theory

Under the learning theory, all of our behaviors are learned as opposed to being innate or instinctual. In other words, the child is born as a blank slate. The child learns different behaviors through conditioning. One form of conditioning has to do with association.

Because the mother is present when the baby gets fed, the baby learns to associate the mother with food. Conditioning can also be involved in behavior. The child learns that by engaging in a specific behavior, the child gets rewarded. An example of this is when the baby smiles and the mother smiles back or kisses the baby.

Because the behavior led to a favorable outcome, the baby will repeat this behavior in the future. Conversely, if the baby engages in a specific behavior that leads to a negative outcome, it will avoid repeating that behavior in the future.

Evolutionary Theory

While learning theory is based on the idea that our attachments to others come about through the process of learning, the evolutionary theory concludes that our need for attachment is hardwired within us from birth. Both Bowlby and Harlow believed that we are born preprogrammed to form attachments to others for the purpose of survival.

Under this theory, infants are born with the means to connect with others. These means come in the form of smiling, crying, and other behaviors that elicit adult nurturing responses. Bowlby believed that the infant forms just one attachment initially and that attachment is with the primary caregiver. It is this attachment that allows the child to explore their world.

This theory suggests that attachments must be formed within the first five years. If an attachment is not made within this period, the child will develop irreversible consequences to its development, such as increased aggression and reduced intelligence. In the next chapter, we look at how attachment styles affect relationships.

CHAPTER 2

How Attachment Styles Affect Relationships

Have you ever reached the point where you gave up on finding that special person who you dreamed of having a relationship with? Perhaps you found yourself falling into a pattern of having relationships with partners who were emotionally exhausting or emotionally unavailable. You may have started to doubt yourself and feel something was wrong with you.

Some researchers believe that our bonding experience with our first relationships, which were with our caregivers, may influence how we relate to intimacy later in life. The four attachment styles can provide us with insight into not only the behavior of our partners but also our own. With this understanding, we can better understand our needs and how to handle the challenges we experience.

Our attachment style influences who we pick as partners and how the relationship will progress. The reason is that our intimate relationships can trigger the attachment styles we adopted as children. In fact, we unconsciously select partners that conform to our attachment styles. We may continue to operate from our attachment styles even though they cause us unhappiness. The following are some examples of relationship patterns that come from an anxious attachment style:

- A tendency to be clingy with one's partner.

- Becoming easily jealous.

- Being more invested in the relationship than one's partner.

- The desire to be with one's partner but backing off when emotional closeness arises.

A person who developed an anxious attachment in childhood is likely to select a partner with an attachment style that mirrors their caregiver's. At an unconscious level, we may select partners that will respond to us as our caregivers did. How we behave in intimate relationships can be governed by our expectations originating from our childhood experiences. In other words, our attachment style can cause us to behave toward our partners in the same way we behaved toward our caregivers as children. The following are ways that our attachment styles impact our adult relationships:

Secure Attachment Style

Those with a secure attachment style develop meaningful relationships where they feel stable and safe. They develop meaningful relationships where they thrive. Further, they establish reasonable boundaries where they thrive and are not afraid to be alone.

It is not that those with a secure attachment style never experience insecurity or that they do not experience relationship problems. The difference is that they feel confident enough to own up to their mistakes and take responsible action to improve things.

Additionally, those with a secure attachment style turn to their partners when they need help or support. The following are characteristics of a relationship when a secure attachment style is involved:

- You recognize your self-worth and can be yourself. Also, you express your needs, feelings, and hopes freely.

- You can enjoy yourself when you are with people other than your partner and are comfortable when you are not with them.

- Not only are you comfortable going to your partner for support, but you are also comfortable with them coming to you when they need to.

- You can manage your emotions and work with your partner to resolve conflict healthily.

- You are resilient enough to bounce back when faced with relationship disappointments or setbacks.

Children with a secure attachment toward their caregivers see them as a source of comfort and security. This security allows them to explore the world around them. In a romantic relationship, this same attachment leads to a similar connection with their intimate partner. This security provides the freedom for partners to live their lives as individuals and as a couple.

Anxious Attachment Style

Someone with an anxious attachment style may be clingy in their relationships and have a continuous need for attention and love. They may be embarrassed by this need. Additionally, they may be emotionally drained by their ongoing concern about whether their partner truly loves them. Other characteristics of the anxious attachment style include:

- You genuinely desire closeness and intimacy with your partner, but you are held back because you do not feel you can trust or rely on them.

- Your intimate relationship consumes your life; your partner is your primary focus.

- You lack boundaries for yourself and frequently violate the boundaries of your partner. Your partner's desire for space threatens you. Situations like this may cause you to experience fear, panic, or anger. These feelings may lead you to believe that your partner is no longer interested in you.

- Your self-esteem is determined by how you feel your partner is treating you. Also, you jump to conclusions and overreact when you perceive a threat to the relationship.

- When you are not with your partner, you become anxious. You may become controlling or make them feel guilty to keep them close.

- You require continuous attention and reassurance from your partner.

- You have difficulty maintaining intimate relationships.

For those with this attachment style, their relationships follow a predictable pattern. The beginning of the relationship is marked by excitement and anticipation of what the relationship could become. There is that first kiss and the anticipation for when they can be with the other person. This relationship stage has an addictive quality, as there is a dopamine release.

At some point in the relationship, it is common for things to level out. The anxious attachment style partner's excitement and anticipation turn into anxiousness or concern. This person will start wondering if their partner is losing interest in them. This sense of doubt puts their partner in a losing position.

Even if their partner gives this person their attention and reassurance, the person with the anxious style attachment will never be satisfied as their hunger is like a bottomless pit. They will continue to believe that their partner is losing interest in them.

This person will engage in thoughts such as:

- Why does my partner not desire me the way that I desire them?

- Why have they not called me? I have not heard from them all day.

- I need to be more attentive to them, and then they will desire me more.

Unlike the authentic bond that secure attached couples enjoy, those with an anxious attachment style strive to fulfill a bond that is built on a fantasy. Rather than experiencing genuine love, their bond is based on an emotional hunger. They look for a partner to rescue or make them feel complete. This approach normally backfires as it causes their partner to back away.

Avoidant Attachment Style

Those with an avoidant attachment style are uncomfortable with emotional intimacy. For these individuals, freedom and independence are very important to them. They feel threatened by intimacy and closeness within a relationship. The following are examples of how an avoidant attachment style affects a romantic relationship:

- A person with this attachment style will be very independent and not feel that they need others.

- They will pull away when their partner tries to get close emotionally.

- If this is your style, you will be uncomfortable expressing your emotions. Your partner may claim that you are being distant. You may counter by accusing them of being needy.

- Those with this attachment style will dismiss their partner's feelings. They also may keep secrets from their partner and have affairs. Having affairs is a way for them to reclaim their sense of freedom.

- They are more comfortable with temporary or casual relationships than intimate and long-term ones. If they seek a relationship, they will be attracted to someone who is also independent. By doing so, they can remain emotionally distant.

- Intellectually, those with an avoidant attachment believe they do not need intimacy. In their hearts, however, they do desire a close and meaningful relationship. They resist this desire because they have a deep fear of intimacy.

Those with this style of attachment focus on their own needs. They want to turn to their partner to meet their needs, but their fear of getting hurt severely handicaps them. They put themselves in a no-win situation and do not get their needs met.

Now that we have covered the main attachment styles and how they affect relationships, we will take a deep dive into the anxious attachment style, which begins in the next chapter.

CHAPTER 3

The Anxious Attachment Style

Before discussing the anxious attachment style, it is useful to consider the importance of attachments. The development of attachments is an evolutionary mechanism to increase the probability of the survival of vulnerable individuals, including children.

The attachment system evolved as a response to the fears or distress of the individual. It promotes survival by promoting proximity between the caregiver and the child. The proximity reduces stress and anxiety in the child and increases its probability of survival so that it can mature and reproduce.

The attachment mechanism remains activated when the child's sense of security is inadequate. As the child grows, it develops a mental record (IWM) of its ability to receive proximity and comfort from its caregiver. This mental record remains with the individual as they advance toward other relationships, including friends, parents, and romantic partners. The individual experiences these other relationships through the same mental record they had with their caregiver.

The mental record is comprised of two parts: a mental record of significant others and a record of one's self. The mental record of significant others contains information on how others responded to the individual when they were in distress. The mental record of one's self contains information on an individual's ability to attract proximity and comfort and one's worth as a partner in the relationship. The need for a sense of security is as real for us today as it was in primordial times.

It is common to experience periods of insecurity within a relationship, fearing that a loved one will leave us. However, this is taken to an extreme for those with an anxious attachment style. For these individuals, the feelings of insecurity and fear of loss are so strong that they take over the relationship.

Those with an anxious attachment style have developed a mental representation of relationships that makes them uncertain whether or not they can count on their partner. This doubt increases their distress and makes them feel even less safe.

As a result, those with an anxious attachment become hyper-vigilant and sensitive toward their partner's responses.

Those with an anxious attachment style have a deep need for acceptance and engage in people-pleasing behaviors. The real cost to those with this attachment style is when their people-pleasing behaviors prevent them from being able to value themselves or recognize their own needs.

All of this sustains or escalates their anxiousness and makes their relationships unsatisfying. Approximately 19% of the population has an anxious attachment style.

How Anxious Attachment Styles are Created

From the time we are infants, we learn that we can get our emotional and physical needs met by our caregivers. When our caregiver is responsive to our needs, we develop a secure attachment style.

The story changes for the child that perceives that it cannot depend on its caregiver to meet its needs. There are times when the caregiver may be loving and responsive. Other times, the caregiver's response may be unloving, or they may ignore the child. When this happens, the child cannot form a secure bond with their caregiver as they receive mixed signals. This unstable relationship creates an anxious attachment style for the child. As with all attachment styles, the anxious attachment style lays the foundation for how the child will experience relationships as it progresses into adulthood.

However, inconsistency by the caregiver is not the only way a child can develop an anxious attachment style. The anxious attachment style can be passed down from generation to generation. Some caregivers have deep emotional neediness. The caregiver depends on the child to fulfill their need for emotional and physical closeness.

These caregivers may act overly intrusive or protective in caring for the child. Their intention is to meet their own need for love, or to create the image that they are the "perfect parent." The caregiver might be unaware of their self-serving behavior if they have been raised the same way by their own parents. The caregiver is unknowingly passing their anxious attachment style on to their child.

An overprotective parent may appear to respond to their child's needs effectively. However, the problem is that the caregiver is responding to their own needs instead of the child's. As with the inconsistent caregiver, the needy caregiver is not meeting the child's needs. Instead, they may behave in a clinging manner toward their child to fill their own emotional void. Not focusing on the needs of the child creates a generational cycle of anxious attachment.

When a caregiver focuses on the child, the child feels safe and cared for. As early as infancy, the child is absorbing information about their experiences with their caregiver. When the child cannot experience the caregiver's attention and calmness, they are left feeling uncertain.

Regardless of the cause, the child internalizes this anxious attachment and brings it into their adult relationships. The cycle continues if they do not work on themselves and then choose to have children.

There are situations where a child can develop an anxious attachment from having a caregiver who has an avoidant attachment style. Because the avoidant parent cannot meet the child's emotional needs, the child grows up and looks to their adult romantic relationships for what they did not get during childhood. In this case, this person unconsciously tries to bring healing to their deprived inner child. However, this never works.

As adults enter a romantic relationship, they will carry the same uncertainty about their partner as they did with their caregiver. In other words, they will doubt their partner will be there for them.

Which Children Are at the Greatest Risk?

The following are the childhood experiences that may increase the probability of developing an anxious attachment style:

- Being separated from the parent or caregiver at an early age.

- Physical or sexual abuse.

- Incidents of mistreatment or neglect.

- Having a caregiver responds with annoyance or ridicule when the child is in distress.

Signs of Anxious Attachment

Style in Children

The following are signs that a child may have an anxious attachment style:

- They become very distressed when they are separated from their parents.

- When they are upset, they are inconsolable. They will not respond to attempts to comfort them.

- They are clingy toward their caregivers.

- They are fearful of strangers.

- They have difficulty forming relationships with other children.

- There is a hesitation to explore their environment.

- Their general appearance is that of being anxious.

- It is difficult for them to regulate or control their negative emotions.

- They behave aggressively.

Signs of Anxious Attachment Style in Adults

The following signs in adults may be due to an anxious attachment style:

- They have low self-esteem and see others as being better than them.

- They are attuned to the needs of their partner but neglect their own.

- If their partner does not meet their needs, they blame themselves and believe they are not worthy of love.

- They need continuous reassurance that they are loved and that they are good enough.

- They can be extremely suspicious or jealous of their partner.

- Their fear of abandonment can lead them to become preoccupied with their relationship.

- They are uncomfortable being alone.

- Low self-esteem.

- The constant need for intimacy and closeness.

- Fear of being abandoned.

- They are overly dependent on their relationship.

- They are people-pleasers, and they constantly need approval.

- It is difficult for them to trust their partner. This lack of trust comes from being unable to depend on their caregiver as a child.

- Being very sensitive toward their partner's moods and actions.

- They fixate or overanalyze minor situations.

- They experience a pattern of not experiencing love in their relationships.

- They are overly attentive to their partner's needs with the motive of wanting their partner to need them.

- They take responsibility for most of the blame and guilt that exist in the relationship.

  The following are examples of anxious attachment style behaviors:

- You text or call your partner repeatedly until you receive a response from them.

- You frequently check their social media accounts.

- You feel suspicious when there is calm in the relationship.

- You participate in whatever activities your friends want, even when you would rather be doing something else.

- You overextend yourself at work by taking on extra projects to please your co-workers.

- You have difficulty saying "no," even when you really want to.

- You continually ask your partner if they find you attractive.

- You will do anything to avoid ending a relationship, even when you know that the relationship is not healthy for you.

Adults with an anxious attachment style believe they have to earn their partners' love and approval, instead of believing they deserve to be loved. As we will see later, this dynamic often causes those with an anxious attachment style to be attracted to those with an avoidant attachment style.

In such relationships, the anxious attached partner has to work for their partner's attention. This kind of relationship feels natural to them. Conversely, they would find it boring to be with a partner who freely gives love and attention.

In the next chapter, we will take a deeper look into how the anxious attachment style impacts relationships.

CHAPTER 4

The Anxious Attachment Style in Relationships

Being in a relationship with someone with an anxious attachment style is like being on an emotional roller coaster. In such relationships, things can be intense and stressful for both partners. The partner with the anxious attachment style can become like a bottomless pit in their need for validation from their partner. Regardless of how often they receive validation from their partner, the partner with this attachment type will continue to anticipate being abandoned.

The mindset that comes with this attachment style leads to a self-fulfilling prophecy. At the subconscious level, such individuals expect to be rejected and will be attracted to individuals who are not emotionally available for a healthy relationship. When this happens, the anxious styled partner will make an extra effort to persuade their partner to stay in the relationship. What often occurs is that the other partner will eventually take advantage of them by treating them badly. This dynamic becomes a vicious cycle.

Even if the partner does not take advantage of the anxious styled individual, they will experience much pressure due to their partner's neediness and are likely to distance themselves from them. For the anxious styled partner, healing comes when they learn to be able to trust that their partner loves and cares about them. Until then, their continuous doubt will most likely lead to a relationship decline.

The following are some characteristics of such relationships:

Clinginess

In the relationship, the person with the anxious attachment style may become fixated on their partner. They are likely to want to rush into the relationship and want their partner to commit to them. These individuals often fall in love quickly and become obsessed with their partners. Additionally, they may look to their partner to fulfill all of their desires, which creates anxiety for both partners.

Long-distance relationships with anxious attachment types are more difficult than with non-attached partners, because it creates great anxiety for them.

Rejection Fears

Those with an anxious attachment continuously fear their partners breaking off the relationship, or not being there for them in their times of need. They are hyper-vigilant and have the mindset that their partner will leave them. Because of this, they are triggered by any sign of disappointment or disagreement with their partner. This ongoing fear is a product of their low self-esteem.

They will blame themselves if their partner does not respond to their needs or rejects them for any reason. Their partner's response will reinforce their belief that they are not worthy of being loved.

Constant Need for Reassurance

It is both normal and healthy to seek reassurance from one's partner. The challenge with anxiously attached individuals is that they are persistent in their need for reassurance. This persistent need can be emotionally draining for their partner as they must continuously prove their love to them.

Emotional Instability

As mentioned earlier, relationships with those who have an anxious attachment style can feel like an emotional rollercoaster. Partners never know what to expect from the anxiously attached person. They may be high or low, filling the relationship with stress and anxiety.

Further, the relationship quality is usually low for both partners. The partner becomes frustrated with the other person's constant need for reassurance, while the person with an anxious attachment will become anxious because of their partner's frustration.

Feelings of Being Unappreciated

Those with an anxious attachment style often feel unappreciated as they do not feel they are getting the love and attention they deserve. The challenge is that their continuous need for reassurance makes it unrealistic for their partner to give them the appreciation that they desire.

It is common for this attachment style to feel unappreciated, which causes them to worry about their place in the relationship. They can become consumed with the thought that their partner does not love them as much as they love their partner. Those with an anxious attachment style may be clinging to a fantasy of how the relationship should be, and they evaluate the relationship based on that fantasy.

They have trouble understanding that relationships are dynamic and that the way the relationship started (the honeymoon state) cannot be expected to last. When the partner no longer treats them as they did at the beginning of the relationship, the anxious attached will become suspicious of their partner. They will likely accuse their partner of not appreciating them or believe they are unworthy of love.

What further makes dealing with anxious attachment partners challenging is that they avoid expressing their feelings, as they fear showing vulnerability. Because they do not express their feelings, they do not get their needs met. In place of expressing their feelings, they act defensively or provocatively.

Those with an anxious attachment style normally have a positive view of others but a negative one of themselves. They tend to overly idealize their romantic relationships, on which they build their self-esteem.

The Dance of Opposites

Those with an anxious attachment style are frequently attracted to people with an avoidant attachment style. As a reminder, those with an avoidant attachment style avoid intimacy.

Why would someone who craves intimacy be attracted to someone who avoids it? The answer is the person who has the anxious attachment has been programmed by their past to expect their partner will not give them the attention they desire. The one with the avoidant attachment style fits the mental model that the anxiously attached person developed with their caregiver.

All couples engage in a psychological dance, where they balance their needs for intimacy. In this dance, one partner moves forward while the other steps back. In other words, one partner wants to move toward emotional intimacy while the other wants to step away from it. The partners do not do this consciously, and they are continuously switching roles.

In a normal relationship, this dance functions to maintain a balance in emotional intimacy. At some point, the partner who advances will retreat, while the partner who retreats will advance.

This dance reflects a dilemma that we all face. We have a conflicting need for both intimacy and autonomy. We also have a fear of being too close and a fear of being abandoned. This is the dilemma that is posed by intimacy.

When an anxious attachment partner enters a relationship with an avoidant style partner, the partners never change roles. The anxious partner is always pursuing, and the avoidant partner is always backing away. One partner is always seeking intimacy, and the other always avoids it.

Those with the anxious attachment style are subconsciously drawn to those who are emotionally unavailable. The person with the anxious attachment will work hard to get their avoidant attached partner to stay with them. However, the avoidant style partner is programmed to avoid intimacy. The avoidant attached partner's behavior validates the fears of the anxiously attached partner that they are unlovable. The dynamics of the relationship create a vicious cycle.

The Origins of Anxious and Avoidant Dance

This dance between anxious and avoidant partners highlights how we can be impacted by our relationship as children with our caregivers. The anxious attachment style is often caused by an emotionally unavailable parent or caregiver. Babies and young children depend on their caregivers to have empathy for them. They need that person to be responsive to their needs and emotions. Through this responsiveness, babies develop a sense of self and wholeness.

For the development of that sense of wholeness to take place, children depend on validation from their caregivers. Unfortunately, that validation may not occur if the caregiver is emotionally unavailable, suffering from illness, or neglects the child for other reasons. If the caregiver lacks self-esteem, is depressed, or is ill, they may lack healthy boundaries between them and the child.

Instead of responding to the child's needs, they will view the child as an extension of themselves. They will view the child as a way to meet their own feelings and needs. The caregiver is unable to view the child as a separate self. As a result, there is a violation of the child's boundaries. The child's thoughts and feelings are disrespected.

As a result, the child is not given a chance to develop a healthy sense of self. Instead, the child learns they must meet the caregiver's needs to gain love and approval. Furthermore, they learn to focus on the caregiver's expectations and responses. The result is that the child develops a sense of shame and codependency. As the child develops, they may lose touch with their thoughts, feelings, and needs.

When the child reaches adulthood, the experience of being separated from an intimate partner awakens those pains and fears from early on. The anxious partner will feel abandoned if the avoidant partner does not meet their needs and feelings. In this case, both partners find themselves in a codependent relationship where neither is a separate and whole person. As a result, there is no emotional intimacy. In its place is the fear of dissolution and subsequent nonexistence.

Relationships: The Mirrors to Our Concealments

Many do not realize that there is a reason why we are drawn to certain people. The people with whom we enter a relationship provide a mirror to our hidden worlds. We try to repress or disown some aspects of ourselves, which we often do unconsciously.

We invite those who are our opposite into our lives. Unconsciously, we do so in the hopes that they will make us feel whole. The individual who has an anxious attachment style is fearful of abandonment. However, they also have a fear of intimacy. This is why those with an anxious attachment style find themselves drawn to those with an avoidant attachment style. The individual with the anxious attachment style is looking to the avoidant partner to create the space needed for them to experience independence and autonomy.

Similarly, the avoidant partner fears becoming trapped. They avoid emotional closeness as that would make them vulnerable. For this reason, they rely on their anxious partner to meet their intimacy needs.

The internal dialogue of the avoidant attachment style goes something like this:

"My partner is too needy, dependent, or emotional."

Simultaneously, they are also asking themselves:

"Am I capable of love, or am I too selfish? It seems that whatever I give it is never enough."

In the case of the anxious partner, they are telling themselves:

"My partner always has to have their way. They are emotionally withdrawn, inconsiderate, and selfish."

Simultaneously, they are asking themselves:

"Is there something wrong with me? Is it that I am not pretty, smart, or successful enough?"

Both partners blame each other and themselves. The anxious partner feels resentful that they are not getting their needs met, while the avoidant partner feels guilty that they are not meeting their partner's needs. However, something even deeper is happening in the minds of this couple.

The anxious partner judges the part of themselves that is independent or selfish, while the avoidant partner judges the part of themselves that is vulnerable, needy, and dependent.

However, both partners are projecting the part of themselves that they cannot accept onto their partner.

In such a relationship, the avoidant partner will push away the anxious partner. In response, the anxious partner will become more determined to connect with the avoidant partner. They may be relentless in their attempts to be with them.

The anxious partner's behavior only emboldens the avoidant partner with the confidence that they can do whatever they want, and the anxious partner will be there waiting for them. This is the playbook by which both partners use to experience intimacy. Both partners need to accept and embrace all aspects of themselves to heal.

The Anxious Attachment Style in the WorkPlace

How attachment styles play out in the workplace has not received much attention from researchers; however, this is changing. There has been more research in this area within the last five years than in the previous 25 years combined. One study involved the social dynamics of attachment theory in the workplace. They studied how attachment style dynamics affected workers and those in leadership positions. Their findings are as follows:

Anxious Attachment Style in Workers

Workers with anxious attachment styles can create conflict in the workplace due to their constant need for approval. Those with this attachment style tend to be highly insecure and have self-doubt, leading to the need for continuous approval from their co-workers.

Because they want to please everyone, they conform to "group think." They also avoid confrontation and are constantly looking to be praised for their work. The challenge in the workplace is that these things become their priority. The result is that the unrealistic expectations and demands that they have for themselves can create an uncomfortable work environment.

Further, those with this attachment style do not function well when working alone. When they are part of a team, they may lean on others for help completing their work. Because of their constant need for approval, they tend to be more sensitive toward constructive feedback, more likely to feel unappreciated, and more likely to be dissatisfied with their jobs. The result of all this is a higher frequency of burnout.

Although the anxious attachment style can pose challenges to the workplace, it also has positive qualities. Those with this attachment style quickly detect workplace threats or risks because of their hyper-vigilance. Additionally, they are very self-reflective and are aware of the areas in which they fall short. This quality, along with their desire to please others, means that they are continuously working on improving themselves.

Finally, this is one attachment style you do not have to worry about being a troublemaker. Because of their desire to belong, they will follow workplace norms. In the next chapter, we will discuss ways to cope with an anxious attachment style.

CHAPTER 5

How to Cope with Your Anxious Attachment Style

The anxious attachment style is not a form of mental illness. It is formed in childhood when our caregivers do not meet our emotional needs. As with the other attachment styles, the anxious attachment style was adopted to cope with this reality. The challenge is that these adaptations no longer support us as we age.

Changing one's attachment style is very difficult because it becomes part of one's personality. Because of this, changing one's attachment style requires constant vigilance. Instead of trying to change one's attachment style, it is more practical to learn how to cope with it and develop a more secure attachment style.

Each of us has the potential to create change in our lives, regardless of age. Anxious attachment styles are the result of our deep-seated beliefs. However, we can change them. Creating a change in our beliefs requires that we challenge them. To do so, however, requires support, practice, and patience. This is because our self-talk, our harshest critic, will hinder our attempts to change.

This voice was developed from our childhood experience and will do its best to keep us from experiencing our emotions. It is the discomfort of these emotions that the insecure attachment styles are designed to save us from.

Fortunately, recognizing one's insecure attachment style is half the battle in creating change. There can be no healing without self-awareness. Understanding one's attachment style lets one know what one must work on. Developing a more secure attachment style is definitely possible regardless of one's insecure attachment style.

Awareness is the organizing principle behind all change, including changes in attachment styles. True healing comes from learning to make sense of how one interacts with others, especially one's partners. By recognizing one's behavioral patterns in relationships, and becoming mindful of them, creating empowering change becomes that much easier. It is for this reason that self-reflection is so important.

Bringing Awareness to Anxious Attachment

Those with an anxious attachment style are normally reactive to what they perceive as a negative situation. In other words, they are on autopilot. They automatically respond to the situation without thinking about it. When we become more aware of how we respond, we can think of more empowering ways to respond.

Coping Strategies for the Anxious Attachment Style

If you have an anxious attachment style, you can develop a more secure attachment pattern by understanding your coping strategies and learning how to respond in more empowering ways. You can begin by asking yourself the following questions:

How do I create closeness in my relationship? Examples of answers to this question include:

- I do not disagree with my partner.

- I act seductively.

- I become my partner's caretaker.

- I engage in people-pleasing behavior.

In my efforts to build closeness, what do I give up? Examples of answers to this question include:

- I give up my autonomy.

- I give up my hobbies and interests.

- I give up my friendships.

- I give up my right to disagree.

When you engage in these behaviors without being aware of them, you aren't doing so by choice, but due to your unconscious thinking patterns. Because of this, you are unable to communicate your needs effectively. Rather, you are unconsciously trying to manipulate your partner. If your partner has an avoidant attachment style, they are doing the same thing to you.

Overcoming the anxious attachment styles involves learning new ways of thinking that support our happiness and being able to connect with others. Though this may sound simple, making such a change takes patience, determination, and persistence. As healthier ways of viewing ourselves and others sink in, the corresponding behaviors and emotions will follow.

Making such a change can be difficult and scary because it requires learning to trust oneself and others, both of which go against the way insecure attachment styles are programmed. However, it can be done! A good place to start is learning about your triggers.

Anxious Attachment Style Triggers

The signs of the anxious attachment style do not appear all the time. Rather, they are triggered by the behaviors of their partners. The following are examples of triggers that can activate the anxious attachment style:

- Arguments

- Inconsistent behavior by a partner.

- The partner arrives home later than expected.

- When the partner seems distracted or distant.

- The partner forgets an important occasion, like an anniversary or birthday.

- Not receiving a call or message from a partner when it was expected.

- The partner fails to notice something important to the individual.

- Their partner does not appear to be paying attention to them because they are involved in a project or activity.

- A breach of trust by the partner.

When this attachment style is triggered, the individual experiences increased self-doubt and insecurity. The following are examples of what the anxiously attached individual may think when hearing the following from their partners:

Partner: "I need some time to be with myself."

Anxious Attached: What did I do wrong? Or, how can I fix the situation?

Partner: "Sorry I did not call you earlier; I was talking to some people I know."

Anxious Attached: Who was he talking to? Why are they more important than me?

Partner: "I need to reschedule our plans. I have to get caught up in my work."

Anxious Attached: My partner is cheating on me. I will not let them get away with this!

Modern Technology as a Trigger

Our modern technology has enormous benefits for us in terms of accessing information and communicating with each other. However, for those of us with an anxious attachment style, technology can also heighten our insecurity. Let's use texting as an example. Texting can compound the feeling of insecurity that people with anxious attachment experience. The following are examples:

- The anxious partner starts to panic when they do not receive a text from their partner to confirm upcoming plans.

- The anxious partner texts someone they are interested in, but that person does not reply.

- The anxious partner receives a reply from their person of interest and scrutinizes it if it does not meet their expectations.

Triggered Behaviors

When we give in to our anxious attachment style, we give into the emotions that come up when we are triggered. The following are examples of triggered behavior:

- Making repeated attempts to connect or reconnect with a partner.

- Withdrawing

- Being hostile

- Keeping score

- Making threats of leaving

- Manipulating others

- Attempting to make your partner jealous.

How to Handle Triggers in Yourself

You can learn to overcome your triggers if you have an anxious attachment style. The following are some suggestions:

Remember to Breathe

One of the most important things you can do is remember to breathe. Focusing on your breathing will ground you in your body and keep you from getting caught up in your emotions.

When you feel triggered, pause and focus on your breath. Notice the sensations that you experience in your body. If you feel stress in your body, do not try to change it. Instead, accept that it exists and focus on your breath and bodily sensations.

Interrupt Your Thoughts

If you feel triggered, interrupt your thought pattern by changing your thinking to something positive. An example of interrupting your thoughts is to think about planning something that you would like to do, such as planning a vacation. Doing this will keep you from running your habitual thought patterns. If you do not engage in your usual thinking, you will not become emotionally excited as easily. Naturally, this method takes consistent practice for it to become effective.

Place Yourself Behind the Wheel

Another method for overcoming your triggers is to place yourself in the driver's seat. Focus on the thought that you are the hero of your own story and are in charge of your happiness. You will gradually learn to be less reactive to your partner by putting yourself in control.

In using any of these suggestions, it is important to note that it takes consistent practice to make a difference. It is also important to remember that you are trying to change a behavior pattern that you have had since you were a child. For these reasons, you are advised to be patient and gracious with yourself and your partner as you learn to change your reactions when triggered.

Awareness of Your Physiology

Triggering the anxious attachment style results in the flight, fight, or freeze response. The flight or fight response is well known. In the face of danger, animals will either flee or defend themselves. The freeze response is something that occurs in this attachment style. The response is one of confusion. The person is unable to think clearly. When this happens, the person will go by their first impulse.

You can remove yourself from the freeze response by taking a moment to breathe. Focus on the sensations of your breath as you breathe. You may also want to place your hands on your abdomen to connect with its movements as it rises and falls.

By doing this, you are redirecting your attention from your thinking and signaling to your brain that you are safe. Also, there are numerous grounding activities that you can do when you feel anxious. Consider exercising, meditating, doing yoga, taking a walk-in nature, or getting a massage.

Learn to Self-Soothe

An important part of moving beyond your anxious attachment style is learning to self-soothe, which is especially important when coping with jealousy. Jealousy is a hallmark of the anxious attachment style. In fact, those with an anxious attachment style will often feel that their feelings are being reciprocated when their partner experiences jealousy.

For anxiously attached partners, jealousy can make them feel closer to their partners. Further, the feeling of jealousy makes them feel more alive. The anxious partner may feel more connected to their partner when they experience jealousy, taking it as a sign that their partner cares about them.

Naturally, this kind of mindset will not lead you to a more secure relationship style. It is important that you deal with your feelings of jealousy; an effective way of doing so is through self-soothing.

Dealing with jealousy through self-soothing starts with understanding that jealousy is usually a coping strategy used when anticipating loss. This fear of loss predates your adult relationships, beginning with your relationship with your primary caregiver. By doing inner child work, you can uncover the original source of your fears and become less reactive toward them.

The process's next step is to understand that jealousy can be used to serve you in your relationships. You allow your partner to experience your vulnerability by becoming honest with your feelings. What can come from this is a deeper connection between you and your partner. Your partner then has the opportunity to meet your needs.

Additionally, getting to know your jealousy can help you gain a deeper understanding of what you need to strengthen your self-esteem. This is because feelings of inadequacy, shame, disrespect, or failure are often the products of jealousy.

By mindfully confronting these products of jealousy, you can experience a broader range of emotions that elevate rather than disempower. The emotion of jealousy is a message that we need to tend to our own needs.

Nurture Your Inner Child

If you have an anxious attachment style, you likely developed it when you were a child. So bringing healing to that child is a great place to start. The term "inner child," refers to the emotional energy created when you were a child but still holds on to you today.

This emotional energy contains the memories of your interactions with your caregiver and the emotional pains you associate with them. So, the inner child is a metaphor, and it continues to influence you by causing you to feel and react today just as you did when you were a child.

Healing your inner child will require you to look within yourself and acknowledge the emotional pain that you experienced. When your emotional pain is recognized, you can then reparent your inner child by providing for its needs.

When working on your inner child, you will face resistance, so gaining your inner child's trust may take time. As you gain your inner child's trust, you can get in touch with what it is feeling.

Gaining your inner child's trust requires consistency on your part. You need to align what you say with what you do. In other words, your behavior needs to be more congruent with how you feel. To do this, it is important that you develop the attitude that you are deserving of what you need and to feel what you feel. This requires you not to allow anyone to keep you from being true to your inner child.

When you claim responsibility for your inner child, you can then commit to loving it. You need to treat your inner child the same way a loving mother treats her infant. You are committed to meeting all of its needs. When doing inner child work, we learn to experience a deep love that is both receiving and giving.

Having learned to care for your inner child, you will need to extend that into your relationship with your partner. This means you must prioritize your needs to balance them with your partner's needs. Further, you will need to learn to stop searching for validation through your partner. You need to learn that the only validation that you need is your own.

Bring Evidence to Faulty Thinking

When experiencing negative thought patterns, it is important to evaluate their truthfulness rather than just blindly accepting them as being accurate. When you experience a negative thought, challenge it.

Look for any evidence that may disprove the thought. For example, you may think that people cannot be trusted. You can challenge that thought by looking back to see if you ever had an encounter with someone who did not betray your trust. You can also explore other possible explanations for your thinking. You may believe someone violated your trust, but is it possible there is another explanation? Could it be that instead of intentionally violating your trust, they made a mistake or were unaware of what they were doing?

By creating a sense of doubt in our negative thinking, we weaken it and provide the opportunity for us to engage in less "black and white" thinking.

Express Yourself

Instead of allowing yourself to be consumed by your thoughts, express your feelings safely and enjoyably. The feelings you experience when anxious can be rendered harmless if you externalize them instead of bottling them up within you.

Find a way to express your feelings through creative means such as art, music, or dance. You can also record them in a journal. Another approach is to journal from the perspective of your inner child. Discover why your inner child is feeling the way they do.

Rehearse Your Script

If you anticipate having an important conversation, prepare for it in advance. Just as an actor practices their lines, you can practice the message you want to give. Make your message honest, kind, and clear so that you do not come across as being controlling or needy.

Get To Know the Secure Attachment Style

Start forming relationships with people who have a secure attachment style. By doing so, you will be able to learn what a secure and stable relationship is like. By doing so, you may be able to interrupt your pattern of going after individuals who have an avoidant attachment style.

Practice Being Vulnerable

To develop a more secure type of attachment, try focusing on being more vulnerable while simultaneously creating emotional safety for yourself. One example is to step out of your comfort zone by clearly expressing how you feel about a situation.

Explicitly state what you want and what you do not want. Learn to clearly express to others your feelings, needs, and desires, even if you are concerned about their reaction.

Associating with people who have a secure attachment style will help you learn how to handle yourself in interpersonal situations where you are assertive but emotionally safe.

Increase Your Emotional Intelligence

Also called emotional quotient (EQ), emotional intelligence is the ability to understand, employ, and manage one's emotions in a way that benefits the relationship. The relationship benefits through greater empathy for one's partner, effective communication, and healthy conflict resolution.

By increasing your emotional intelligence, you can also express your needs more effectively to your partner and improve your understanding of how your partner feels.

Deal with Childhood Trauma

As mentioned earlier, childhood trauma can lead to an insecure attachment style by disrupting the attachment process. Childhood trauma can include any situation that threatens your sense of security as a child. Such situations may include an unstable or unsafe home environment, separation from your primary caregiver, or experiencing abuse, neglect, or serious illness. When our childhood trauma is not addressed, the feelings of fear, insecurity, and helplessness may be carried over into adulthood.

Taking Time for Yourself

Each day, take time for self-care. It is important that you do this consistently. In other words, make it part of your daily routine. Doing this will help calm your anxiety. Take time to do those things that you enjoy and find relaxing.

Strengthen Your Nonverbal Communication

The source of our attachment styles was our nonverbal communication with our primary caregiver when we were very young. Just as nonverbal communication determines the success of our relationship with our primary caregiver, it also plays a big role in determining the success of our adult relationships.

Though we may not be aware of it, we continuously give nonverbal signals as we interact with others. These nonverbal signals include things like our posture and eye contact. These signals communicate how we feel about a situation.

We can strengthen our relationships with others by learning to interpret and communicate non-verbally. You can develop this skill by learning to be present in the moment, managing stress, and developing greater emotional awareness. All of these things can be developed through the practice of mindfulness.

Practice Mindfulness

One of the challenges that many of us experience is that we overanalyze things and often do so from a negative perspective. This is especially true for those with an anxious attachment style. By practicing mindfulness, you can learn to focus on the present moment and manage any uncomfortable emotions in a way that empowers you.

Being present will make you feel more confident when interacting with others and develop greater confidence in the relationship. There are different ways to practice mindfulness, some include:

- Meditation

- Tai chi

- Yoga

- Walking meditation

- Gardening

Therapy

Getting therapy is very helpful for learning how to cope with anxious attachment styles. It will allow you to be in a safe place to explore thoughts and feelings and learn new and empowering ways to engage with others. Cognitive behavioral therapy (CBT) has been shown to be effective for identifying and changing negative thoughts and behavior patterns.

Another way to become more effective in interpersonal relationships and social interactions is through Interpersonal therapy (IPT). Psychodynamic psychotherapy is useful for recognizing how your emotions impact you at the subconscious level.

It is important to note that having an anxious attachment style does not mean something is wrong with you. Rather, you have learned a way to navigate relationships that most likely are not serving you in becoming fulfilled emotionally.

By understanding how your attachment style impacts you in your relationships, you can begin the process of learning how to manage it. Self-awareness and communication are key to managing thoughts and behaviors associated with this attachment style. This involves becoming aware of your attachment style and learning how to express what you are feeling.

Next time you feel triggered, examine how you are feeling at that moment and what you are thinking. Ask yourself what is the meaning that you are giving to the situation. If you do this, you will no longer be going on autopilot. You will be able to think of healthier ways to respond to the situation.

If you find this too difficult, you can remove yourself from the situation before responding. Find a place where you feel safe so that you can gather your thoughts before you go back to the situation.

In the next chapter, we will continue to explore ways to deal with this attachment style within the context of a relationship.

CHAPTER 6

The Anxious Attachment Style, Partners, and Dating

Whether you have an anxious attachment style or your partner does, there are things that you can do to improve the quality of the relationship. In this chapter, we will explore what you can do if you are dating, already in a relationship, and how you can support a partner who has an anxious attachment style. Though divided into sections, the suggestions listed are useful in all cases.

Dating and Anxious Attachment Style

You can take steps to prepare yourself better when dating or entering a relationship. As with the other suggestions in this chapter, these steps involve developing greater clarity about yourself and what you need. It all begins with your values.

Know Your Values and Needs

Take time to reflect on what you need from a relationship. If you have difficulty answering this question, it is important that you clarify this for yourself. If you are unclear about your needs, how will you or anyone else ever meet them?

You can begin identifying your needs by thinking about your past relationships and making a list of your criticisms. When you have completed your list, review the list from the perspective of your needs. For example, if one of your criticisms was that your previous partners did not make you feel appreciated, one of your needs may be feeling appreciated.

Besides looking at your unmet needs, look for patterns in your past relationships that did not support your happiness. Examples of this are long-distance relationships or relationships where your partners had difficulty expressing themselves. By doing this, you can distinguish between the patterns that worked for you and patterns that you did not need. You can then look for these patterns in the people you meet later on.

Break Your Pattern of Who You Date

As mentioned before, those with an anxious attachment style tend to gravitate toward individuals with an avoidant attachment style. Both the anxious attachment style and the avoidant attachment style are classified as insecure attachments. However, they have opposite needs.

The anxious attachment style craves reassurance and closeness, while the avoidant style seeks autonomy and space. The relationship dynamics are unlikely to change unless both partners desire to change. If you have an anxious attachment style, you would be better off seeking a relationship with someone with a secure attachment style.

Current Relationships and the Anxious Attachment Style

If you are already in a relationship, the following are suggestions for improving your relationship with your partner:

The Languages of Love

In his book, *the Five Love Languages,* Dr. Gary Chapman offers a useful tool for gaining clarification of your needs. Chapman discusses the five love languages. A love language is a specific way to express our love more effectively to others.

Each person has their own language of love. If you understand your partner's love language, they will more likely feel loved. The following are the five love languages:

Words of Affirmation: In this love language, you feel loved when you hear your partner compliment you or express their feelings for you.

Physical Touch: You feel loved when your partner touches you in this love language.

Quality Time: In this love language, you feel loved when your partner gives you their undivided attention or when they spend time with you.

Acts of Service: In this love language, you feel loved when your partner does something on your behalf.

Gifts: In this love language, you feel loved when your partner buys you or makes you something.

It is important to note that we may feel loved by all five of these languages; however, there is one language that is our main language. In other words, each person has one or more love languages that impact them most. If you know your love language, you can let your partner know it is one of your needs. Similarly, if you know your partner's love language, you can meet theirs.

How to Communicate Your Needs to Your Partner

You must communicate your needs to your partner early on in the relationship. It is also important that you communicate your needs clearly. The clearer you are in your communication, the more likely they will meet your needs. Additionally, communicating your needs early in the relationship increases your chances of determining if they are the right person for you.

If communication is important to you, let them know that and then see if they deliver on that.

If receiving compliments and reassurance is important to you, let them know that and see if they follow through. If it is important for you to know when you will see them next, tell them that and see if they will give you an answer. When you do this, you are letting them know what is important to you and seeing if they care enough to put in the effort to meet your needs.

Practice the Art of Detachment

The driving force of the anxious attachment style is to cling and hold on to their partner. What more powerful way could there be to deal with this attachment style than by doing the direct opposite? Why not try a Buddhist approach by following the principle of detachment?

If you have an anxious attachment style, you will likely spend a lot of time thinking about your relationship. However, much of what you think about is probably not in your control. These thoughts will likely trigger your attachment system, leading to fear and a need to cling to the relationship.

When practicing detachment, one does the opposite. Instead of being overwhelmed with fear and needing control, practicing detachment leads to being aware of the present moment without trying to control or resist anything. When practicing detachment, one shifts their attention from what cannot be controlled to what can be, which is ourselves. Great peace comes from experiencing the present moment with complete acceptance.

The principle of detachment is based on the idea that the only ones that we are responsible for are ourselves. We are unable to change anyone except ourselves. Detachment calls us to let life unfold without us trying to force or control the situation. You can begin to practice detachment by becoming aware of the emotions you experience when reacting to a situation.

The emotions you are experiencing are natural; they originate from the past but appear in the present. They do not come from what is happening outside yourself. Rather, they are of your creation and brought back to life when you are triggered.

Accept them as yours and take responsibility for them. You can take responsibility for them by deciding whether or not you will respond to them by taking action. Your emotions are neither good nor bad, for it is you who gives meaning to your emotions. With this in mind, the emotions that you experience can serve you. They are pointing out to you that there are unresolved issues from your past, and they are unresolved because you have not yet taken responsibility for them. To take responsibility for your emotions is to accept them and embrace them while realizing that they have no power over you, though they may feel that way.

The following are ways to remind yourself to stay detached from your emotions:

- How others treat me reflects their character, not mine.

- I have faith that everything will work out as it is intended to. Whatever happens, it is for the best.

- I do not have to deal with that today. I can wait until it is the right time for me.

- I can choose to let go and let things be.

- Whatever happens today was meant to happen. I will not struggle against the workings of the universe.

- If it is meant to happen to me, it will happen.

Turn to Your Creativity

Getting involved with your creativity is a great outlet for exercising your focus while calming your mind. If you feel anxious, turn to express yourself creatively by painting, drawing, coloring, singing, or writing.

Make Use of Your Support System

If you are becoming anxious, talk to a loved one or close friend. Sharing your feelings with others creates a win-win situation. You win by being able to unload what you are feeling, while they win by being allowed to express their compassion and support for you.

All these suggestions share in common that they provide an indirect means to getting your emotional needs taken care of. By doing so, you can get into a calmer state where you can more effectively communicate your needs to your partner. When we do not let others know what we need from them, we deny ourselves. Instead of reacting to your emotions, try to do the following:

1. Objectively describe to your partner what you experienced.

2. Explain to them how it made you feel.

3. When speaking to them, resort to "I" statements rather than "you."

4. While speaking to them, keep an even-toned voice. Avoid getting angry, yelling, or speaking over them.

The following is an example:

"I have not heard from you in a while, and I have a need to be honest with you. I feel anxious when we let days go by without speaking. Are you available to talk today? It would really mean a lot to me."

When phrased this way, you treat yourself and your partner with dignity.

What Would They Do?

It has been mentioned earlier that forming a relationship with someone who has a secure attachment style can help you develop a more secure attachment style. Next time you experience anxiety about your relationship, ask yourself this question, "What would someone with a secure attachment style do in this situation?" By asking this question, you are reframing the situation, allowing you to see it from a different perspective.

What You Can Do for an Anxiously Attached Partner

If you are in a relationship with an anxiously attached partner, the following are some suggestions on how you can support them:

Learn About Their Style

Learn about your partner's attachment style. The more you know about it, the better you will be equipped to understand them.

Don't Show Them…Tell Them

You will be more effective in showing gratitude to your partner if you tell them instead of showing them through your actions. The reason why is that those with this attachment style may not pick up on your intent unless you tell them. When expressing your appreciation to them, begin your statement with "Thank you for…" or "I appreciate that you…."

Knowing What to Say and Not to Say

To more effectively communicate with an anxious style partner, here are some examples of what not to say or do:

- "I am sorry that you feel that way."

- "Why are you so upset? It is no big deal!"

- "I need time to be alone to think."

- "I do not know how I feel; I am just not feeling the chemistry between us."

- "You are overreacting!"

- Give the attached partner the silent treatment.

Doing these things will make your partner feel like you are dismissing their feelings, and it may trigger them. The following are examples of what to say or do:

- "It will be alright; we will somehow get through this."

- "Let me give you a hug; everything will be alright."

- "I am not afraid of your feelings; I want you to tell me how you feel."

- "I may not understand why you feel this way, but I do know what it feels like to be overwhelmed. What can I do to be there for you?"

- Verify that you understand what they are saying and tell them it is important to you.

- Let them cry and hold them.

- Assure them that you care about them.

- Be consistent in giving them your attention.

- Follow through with your commitments and promises.

- Encourage them to engage in techniques of self-awareness and self-reflection.

Making statements and actions like these will pave the way to move beyond the conflict and find common ground. A partner with an anxious attachment style will likely be filled with self-doubt and frequently seek reassurance. For this reason, it is important to tell them how you feel about them rather than assume they know how you feel. It can also be very helpful to tell them how much you value them and your commitment to the relationship and that you are willing to accommodate their needs.

Keep Your Word

Being distrustful of others is an essential characteristic of this attachment style. It is important to keep your promise to your partner and follow through with what you tell them. For your sake, it is also important that you form clear boundaries for yourself and that your partner knows your expectations. Having said this, it is important that you consistently enforce your boundaries and expectations. It is this kind of consistency that will create trust in your partner.

Couples Therapy

Couples therapy can be valuable for both partners. The therapist will be a moderator and support you and your partner in communicating your feelings for each other. The two of you will also learn new communication tools.

What to do if you are in an Anxious and Avoidant Relationship

As noted before, when an anxious individual enters a relationship with an avoidant partner, they will feed off each other's weaknesses. Unless both partners are willing to change, their cycle of dysfunction will continue.

To bring about change, both partners need to follow the same course of action. They need to become conscious of their needs and feelings and be willing to risk what they fear the most.

To bring about change requires that they become conscious of their coping behaviors and resist their compulsions to cling to or avoid each other. To do all of this takes a great deal of courage.

In place of their old ways of relating to each other, the couple needs to learn to acknowledge and accept the emotions that come about when they feel stressed by the relationship. Needless to say, this kind of endeavor should be done with a trained therapist as it can be a difficult journey, especially in the beginning.

When difficult emotions arise, they may trigger feelings of rage, despair, terror, shame, and emptiness. A therapist can help you navigate these emotions and keep them apart from your current circumstances as an adult whose emotional survival is no longer at risk. As the partners work through their feelings, they will become less reactive toward them and develop a more solid sense of self.

By the couple developing and understanding their attachment styles, they learn from each other and learn to embrace the parts of themselves that they had repressed. The anxious partner can learn to set limits for themselves and care for their own needs. In contrast, the avoidant partner can learn to become more adaptable, reach out to others, and empathize with others' feelings.

The anxious partner can learn to say "no," and reduce the impact of separation anxiety, while the avoidant partner can learn to express their feelings to their partner. Ultimately, each partner learns to take responsibility for themselves. They learn to listen to each other empathetically while respecting their own needs and negotiating an agreement. In other words, they learn to compromise.

If you do not have the cooperation of your partner, there are things that you can do as an individual. Start focusing on yourself by getting to know who you are. Get to know your fears and insecurities and embrace them. Instead of seeing them as flaws, learn how you can use them to your benefit. This exploration can be done through professional therapy, meditation, or journaling. In the next chapter, we will examine some studies on the anxious attachment style.

Chapter 7

Research on the Anxious Attachment Style

The following are some studies that have been conducted on the anxious attachment style. Their results can provide insight into how you can better cope with your attachment style.

Gratitude: A New Way to Deal with Anxious Attachment?

The driving force behind the anxious attachment style is the fear of abandonment. This fear leads to thoughts and behaviors that undercut the building of trust and emotional intimacy. With that in mind, German researchers may have found a valuable tool for overcoming the destructive influences of this attachment style. That tool is gratitude.

Researchers studied the results from a long-term study that tracked romantic couples yearly for a period of over seven years. The study measured the anxiety attachment among couples by asking them to rate their level of agreement with various statements, such as:

- Sometimes, I think my partner does not enjoy being with me as much as I enjoy being with them.

- I frequently think that my partner thinks less of me when I make a mistake.

They also measured the couple's level of gratitude for each other by asking them questions like:

- How frequently does your partner recognize you for what you have done?

- How frequently does your partner express their appreciation for you?

Besides these questions, the couples were also rated on their overall satisfaction with their relationship.

The researchers set out to see if there was a change in these factors over time. What they found surprised them. Partners who measured high for the anxiety attachment style experienced a significant decline in anxiety from a year later. What led to the decline was the experience of gratitude from their partners. But that was not all. The researchers also found that the reverse was not true. Lower levels of anxiety were not a predictor of increased gratitude later on.

The studies suggest that gratitude plays a role in reducing stress within a relationship caused by an anxious attachment style. The researchers believe that partners with an anxious attachment style develop a sense of self-worth and competence when they receive appreciation and recognition from their partners.

A partner's acts of kindness can meet the needs of an anxious partner by making them feel that they are valued in the relationship. The researchers concluded that other factors may have played a role in reducing anxiety; however, these changes were not simply the result of the partners feeling more satisfied with each other. Whether relationship satisfaction increased or decreased, the receiving of their partner's gratitude created a decline in stress in the anxious partner.

This study supports one of the recommendations by experts for changing

an anxious attachment style, which is to form a relationship with someone with a secure attachment style. Those with a secure attachment style have the confidence to share their feelings and express love and affection. So, if you have a partner who has an anxious attachment style, make sure to express your gratitude for them, as long as it is sincere.

The Research: It Does Not Take Much!

Studies have shown that a change in attachment style can occur through positive experiences of closeness and intimacy. One study involved 70 heterosexual couples who participated in a survey regarding their relationship. The couples were then placed into two groups. The first group engaged in activities that promoted greater intimacy and closeness.

These couples took turns answering a series of questions about themselves. The questions selected by the researchers had been proven to enhance feelings of closeness. Another activity this group got involved in was partner yoga, a form of yoga that involved holding hands or other forms of physical contact while creating poses.

The second group engaged in activities that involved answering impersonal questions and individual yoga. After completing their exercises, the participants assessed the quality of their relationships.

Those in the first group, who were identified as having an avoidant style, rated the quality of their relationship higher than they did before participating in the activities. Those who were identified as having a secure or anxious attachment style did not show any change in how they perceived their relationship. This study appears to show that activities that build intimacy may be a benefit for those with an avoidant attachment style.

What is remarkable is that there was a follow-up on the participants one month later. The increase in the satisfaction that the avoidant style participants reported was still there. The study also revealed similar results in couples engaged in spontaneous home interactions. In this study, 67 heterosexual couples in a long-term relationship were asked to keep a diary daily for three weeks. They were told to record their feelings and their partner's behavior toward them.

The study's results found that when the romantic partners of the participants behaved positively toward them, they experienced positive emotions more frequently and negative ones less frequently. They were also happier about their relationship. Positive behaviors by the romantic partners included loving behaviors and listening to the other partner.

These findings were most evident in participants with an avoidant attachment. These studies suggest that those with an avoidant attachment style are more likely to benefit from a positive relationship than the other insecure styles.

What is encouraging about these studies is that they show that a shift to a more secure attachment style can take place by taking action that involves little time or effort. Another study found that those with an avoidant attachment style could reduce the magnitude of their negative emotions by just reflecting on positive relationship memories.

For those with an anxious attachment style, forming a relationship with someone with a secure attachment style has been beneficial in developing a more secure attachment style. Also, healing oneself from codependency is important in achieving a more secure style.

Suggested areas to work on for those with an anxious attachment style include:

- Overcoming feelings of shame and improving your self-esteem.

  Doing these things will keep you from personalizing others' actions of behaviors.

- Learning to become assertive.

- Learning to identify and honor the emotions you experience. Also, learn to express your emotional needs assertively.

- Develop the courage to risk being authentic and direct with your partner instead of playing games or manipulating them.

- Learning to accept others and yourself instead of focusing on the flaws.

- Learning what your triggers are and how to manage them.

- Learn to self-soothe. There are many resources on how to nurture yourself.

- Learn how to compromise and deal with conflict in a way that offers a win-win solution.

Those with an anxious attachment style should become more responsible for themselves. It is recommended that they engage in self-care and learn to nurture themselves. Also important is that they learn to take things slow when dating.

Those who are avoidant would do well to become more attentive to their partner's needs. It would be valuable for them to reveal their vulnerability, acknowledge their need for love, learn to receive, and set their boundaries verbally. Working on these things will cultivate a more secure and interdependent relationship.

It is important to point out that creating change for both insecure attachment styles means facing the fear of becoming dependent on someone. This is especially true after ending a codependent relationship. However, such fears normally come from being in a codependent relationship where neither partner has a secure attachment. A healthy dependency leads to greater interdependence by entering a secure relationship.

The fear of becoming dependent on another person can also arise when seeking therapy. In this case, it is the fear of becoming dependent on the therapist. If you experience this, you would be wise to address this fear with your therapist, as this would be a teaching moment to learn how to manage your fear.

Addressing the fear of dependency with a therapist offers the opportunity to develop the skills needed to handle such situations if they arise in the future with a partner. It is here that the paradox lies. Rather than becoming more dependent, quality therapy can help the individual develop a more secure attachment style, leading to greater autonomy. The greater our own autonomy, the more we will be able of becoming emotionally intimate with others.

Can You Change Your Attachment Style?

Can you change your attachment style? The answer to that question appears to be "no" and "yes." The literature agrees that we cannot change from one style to another; however, we can alter our attachment style to become more or less secure.

The following are three scenarios that illustrate how a life situation can change one's attachment style:

Scenario 1:

A child grows up in a loving and supportive home and develops a secure attachment style. Having a secure attachment style, he learns to trust others and is comfortable with emotional intimacy.

When he gets older, he starts to date. Unfortunately, he experiences a series of disappointing and unhealthy relationships. His partners have insecure attachment styles. They cheat on him, lie to him, or monitor his communications on his social media accounts and cell phone.

Repeated relationships of this kind destroy his confidence, resulting in him adopting a more insecure attachment style. He moves toward the avoidant end of the attachment style spectrum.

Scenario 2:

A woman has an anxious attachment style and is in a relationship where she always feels like she is on shaky ground. She forever fears that her partner will leave or that he is cheating on her. The relationship eventually breaks up. Tired of living this way, she gets therapy and works on herself.

Her efforts pay off, and she meets someone new. Her relationship with her new partner is more characteristic of a secure attachment style. She rarely experiences feelings of anxiety or jealousy. When she does, she knows how to deal with it healthily.

Scenario 3:

A man has an anxious attachment style. Because of this, his relationships are characterized by the constant need for validation from his partners. He decides to go to therapy and spends a lot of time working on himself. Later, he enters a new relationship. He eventually realizes his partner has an insecure attachment style. Instead of reverting to his anxious attachment style, he interacts with his partner more securely.

Research also shows that attachments may change over time as we get older. It is theorized that as we age, we tend to have a lower tolerance for relationships that do not meet our needs, as we have less time. Conversely, major life events can cause a secure attachment style to change to an insecure style. Examples of such events include divorce, loss of a child, and major accidents.

Image of Self and Others

Psychologists have developed a hypothetical model that demonstrates how our attachment style relates to our self-image and the image that we have of others. Those with a secure attachment style have a positive self-image and tend to view others positively.

Those with an anxious attachment style generally have a negative self-image but have a positive perception of others. This causes them to engage in needy behaviors. Individuals with an avoidant attachment style have a positive image of themselves but hold a negative one of others. This is demonstrated by an arrogant attitude and fear of commitment.

Researchers believe that these models can be helpful to those with an insecure attachment to navigate toward a more secure attachment style. The following are examples:

1. Those with an anxious attachment style can work on themselves by building a more positive image and creating healthy boundaries for themselves.

2. For those who are dating, discover what you are passionate about, or look toward what you are good at. Make these things your focus instead of dating. By making these adjustments, you will develop

greater awareness of the self-image of those you date. You will be better equipped to find people to date who are healthier for you.

3. Research shows that those with an anxious attachment style are more likely to make empowering changes when they surround themselves with healthy relationships that provide a positive emotional experience. This is particularly true when the relationship is a significant one, such as a spouse. Such relationship changes can reshape the anxious type's view of the world, reduce their anxiety, and model what a secure attachment style looks like.

The next chapter contains guided meditations and affirmations to assist you in reaching a more secure attachment style.

CHAPTER 8

Guided Meditations and Affirmations

Going from an anxious attachment style to one that is more secure entails creating a new mindset where you have more empowering beliefs about yourself and others. Meditation is a powerful tool for reprogramming your mind to achieve such a mindset.

About Meditation

The purpose of meditation is to redirect your attention from the outer world and toward the inner world. Your experience of the world around you is a projection of how you experience your inner one. By changing your inner experience, you will experience a change in how you perceive yourself and others.

In its purest form, meditation involves going within and silently observing one's mental activity, including thoughts, perceptions, and sensations. Through this silent observation, one develops greater discernment about the nature of one's mental activity and sense of self.

When meditating, one learns how to navigate thoughts and emotions without getting caught up in them. Doing this is liberating as we no longer give our unquestioned allegiance to what our minds tell us.

There are some key points to keep in mind when learning how to meditate:

1. Maintain an attitude of total acceptance and non-judgment for everything you experience.

2. Do not try to control, change, or resist anything you experience.

3. Allow all that you experience the complete freedom to express itself.

4. When meditating, you may experience thoughts such as:

   a. My thoughts keep coming; they are not slowing down.

   b. This is too difficult.

   c. This is boring.

   d. I have more important things to do.

   e. This is not working.

   f. Am I doing this right?

Ignore these thoughts and continue to focus on meditation.

What is Guided Meditation?

Guided meditation is a meditation that follows guidance or a script. Unlike regular meditation, guided meditation guides you to a specific outcome. In other words, guided meditation is like meditation with guardrails to keep you going in a specific direction. In the case of this book, that direction leads toward developing a more secure attachment style!

Requirements: To listen to the guided meditation and receive the full benefits, you will need to download the audio version of this book on Audible. You may alternatively record the script with your own voice on your phone by reciting the words in a calming tone and following the pauses.

Guided Meditation: Before Getting Started

Guided meditation leads you on a journey within. Think of any guidance you receive as a sign on the road. The sign is not the destination; it only serves as a pointer of which direction to go. Far more important than any guidance is what you experience. What you experience while practicing is ultimately what's most important.

You may ask yourself, "But what am I supposed to be experiencing?" The answer to this question is simple. Whatever you are experiencing at any given moment is what you are supposed to be experiencing. This statement is illuminated by the following guidelines for learning to meditate:

- Have unconditional acceptance of anything that you experience. This means that you do not try to change, modify, or resist anything that appears in your awareness. Accept all thoughts, perceptions, and sensations that you experience. Yes, even if your thoughts are racing, let them be. Do not try to control them.

- Do not have any expectations about what you should be or should not be experiencing. Fully accept both yourself and what you are experiencing.

People have trouble meditating mainly because they lack acceptance of what is happening and attempt to control their minds. Instead, be like a birdwatcher observing a rare bird. For the birdwatcher, just observing the bird is a privilege.

A good bird watcher does not intrude on the bird being observed. The birdwatcher allows the bird to behave freely on its own accord. As one who is learning to meditate, you are the bird watcher. What you are experiencing is the bird. You will now start with the first guided meditation, which addresses the body's sensations.

Mindfulness of the Sensations of the Body

Our bodies experience innumerable sensations. Because we are so distracted in our daily lives, we are often unaware of them. Those of us with an anxious attachment style are often unaware of our bodily sensations until we are triggered by something. When this happens, we often get caught up in the unpleasant sensations, which leads us to lose ourselves in our emotions. This mindfulness exercise will help you develop greater awareness of the sensations of your body.

1. Lie down on the floor or on a mat (Using your bed for this exercise is discouraged as you may fall asleep.) **Pause 5 seconds**

2. Place your attention on the movement of your breath as you inhale and exhale.

Pause 3 seconds

3. As you follow your breath, become aware of the sensations of your body. Do you detect a tingling in your feet or hands? Do you sense pressure or stiffness in your back, shoulders, or neck?

4. Allow yourself to experience every sensation that you are aware of. Do not try to change them, ignore them, or judge them as being good or bad. Simply allow yourself to experience them.

Pause 3 seconds

5. Notice that the sensations you feel are not stable as they constantly change in their degree of intensity. In contrast, some sensations may seem to appear, disappear, and then reappear.

Pause 3 seconds

6. Allow yourself to experience any given sensation for as long as you desire. When you are ready, just move on to another sensation. Be

sure to continue breathing as you perform this exercise.

Pause 10 seconds

7. Continue to practice this exercise as long as you wish.

By practicing this meditation, you will develop greater awareness of your body's sensations. By becoming more aware of your sensations, you avoid getting caught up in them as you will not be caught off guard.

Guided Meditation for Relaxing

Just as it is important to be aware of the sensations of your body, it is also important to know how to enter a relaxed state. Knowing how to enter a relaxed state can lower your anxiety level.

1. Take a deep breath and slowly let it out.

    Pause 3 seconds

2. Take another deep breath and slowly let it out.

    Pause 3 seconds

3. Now take a third deep breath. Hold it. Now exhale slowly.

    Pause 3 seconds

4. Now breathe normally.

    Pause 3 seconds

5. Imagine that you are on a cruise liner. You are on vacation, which is long overdue. You have worked hard for so long; now it is your time to escape.

    Pause 5 seconds

6. You are standing at the ship's bow, which is out at sea. All you can see is the vastness of the ocean and the open horizon beyond it.

Pause 5 seconds

7. In your mind, see the endless waves that approach you and hear the gentle hum of the ship's engine.

Pause 3 seconds

8. Sea birds hover above you, and you see an occasional dolphin leap above the waves.

9. The sights and sounds are making you feel more and more relaxed.

10. The gentle ocean breeze and salt spray leave you feeling refreshed and revived.

Pause 3 seconds

11. Take a deep breath and slowly let it out.

Pause 3 seconds

12. Now breathe normally.

Pause 3 seconds

13. Your ship is approaching its destination, an island that few know about.

14. You can see the island in the distance. The captain has informed you that this island will be your "escape from everything" and that you can spend a full day there.

15. What do you say to yourself, knowing that you are leaving the rest of the world behind you?

Pause 3 seconds

16. Take a deep breath and slowly let it out.

Pause 3 seconds

17. Now breathe normally.

Pause 3 seconds

18. Your ship is now anchored less than a mile away from the island. It is the closest that it can get because of the reefs. You board a skiff, and it takes you to the island.

19. When the skiff reaches the island, you disembark. You find yourself on a pristine and secluded beach.

20. Walking along the shore, you realize you are the only one there. There is no one around to distract you from the natural beauty surrounding you.

Pause 3 seconds

21. Feel your toes sink into the soft white sand and the sensations of the surf against your skin.

Pause 3 seconds

22. You keep on walking until you find the perfect spot to lay down your towel and do some sunbathing.

Pause 3 seconds

23. Feel the weight of your outstretched body settle on the softness of your towel and the sand.

Pause 3 seconds

24. Closing your eyes, you hear the soothing sound of the surf as it rushes up the shoreline and the occasional squawking of a seabird.

25. You feel yourself becoming more and more relaxed with the sound of each wave that reaches the shore.

Pause 3 seconds

26. Take a deep breath and slowly let it out.

Pause 3 seconds

27. Now breathe normally.

Pause 3 seconds

28. In your mind, hear the sound of a wave. As you do so, feel your body becoming more relaxed.

Pause 3 seconds

29. Another wave arrives. Feel the stress leave your body as your thoughts evaporate under the sun.

Pause 3 seconds

30. Another wave approaches and feel yourself going deeper and deeper into relaxation.

Pause 3 seconds

31. Notice that your breathing is becoming deeper and fuller.

Pause 3 seconds

32. Feeling fully relaxed, you get up from your towel and walk toward the shore.

33. You wade into the surf and feel the warm turquoise waters against your skin.

34. While bathing in the tropical waters, you look around.

35. In your mind, see the lush green jungles further up the beach.

36. See the endless blue horizon as you look out toward the sea.

37. Notice how free your body feels as the warm, clear waters support you.

Pause 3 seconds

38. Now, take a deep breath and slowly let it out.

Pause 3 seconds

39. Take another deep breath and slowly let it out.

Pause 3 seconds

40. How does it feel to be in a deeply relaxed state?

Pause 3 seconds

41. What do you notice when you are feeling relaxed?

42. Do you feel a certain sensation in your body?

43. How does that sensation feel?

Pause 3 seconds

44. What do you say to yourself when you are feeling very relaxed? Perhaps you do not tell yourself anything, which is very good!

Pause 3 seconds

45. Now take a third deep breath. Hold it. Now exhale slowly.

Pause 3 seconds

46. Now breathe normally.

Pause 3 seconds

47. Though you may imagine that you are on a tropical island, the relaxation you experienced was created by you.

48. Know that you can relax by focusing on anything that you find peaceful.

To be good at anything in life takes practice. Getting what you want out of this meditation is no different. The more you practice this meditation, the greater the results that you experience. For this reason, it is recommended that you meditate daily.

Guided Meditation for Managing Your Emotions

It was previously explained that nothing in our experience has inherent meaning. Instead, it is we who give meaning to our experience. Emotions have a powerful effect on our lives. However, this is made possible only because we grant emotions their power. Because we are the creator of meaning in our lives, we can control the meaning we give to our experiences. The following technique can be used to manage how you feel about a situation.

Guided Meditation for Gaining Control of Negative Emotions

Emotions are a natural aspect of who we are as human beings. Emotions are forms of energy that we have come to categorize as being positive or negative. Unfortunately, many of us focus on our negative emotions. Focusing on our negative emotions can lead to both mental and physical problems. In this meditation, you will be guided to understand better emotions and how to become less reactive to them.

1. Get in a comfortable position and close your eyes.

   Pause 3 seconds

2. Now, take a deep breath and hold it.

    Pause 3 seconds

3. Slowly let it out.

    Pause 3 seconds

4. Breathe normally, and relax.

    Pause 5 seconds

5. Take another deep breath. Hold it.

    Pause 5 seconds

6. Slowly let it out.

    Pause 3 seconds

7. Breathe normally, and relax.

    Pause 3 seconds

8. Take another deep breath. Hold it.

    Pause 5 seconds

9. Slowly let it out.

    Pause 3 seconds

10. Breathe normally, and relax.

    Pause 3 seconds

11. Place your attention on your breath. Make your breath the focus of your attention. Feel the sensations you experience as your breath travels in and out of your body.

Pause 5 seconds

12. Before starting this meditation, you will be guided into deeper levels of relaxation. You will hear a countdown from 10 to 1.

13. As you hear the numbers, notice and focus on the rising and falling of your abdomen as you breathe.

Pause 3 seconds

14. 10

Brief pause

15. 9

Brief pause

16. 8

Brief pause

17. 7

Brief pause

18. 6

Brief pause

19. 5

Brief pause

20. 4

Brief pause

21. 3

Brief pause

22. 2

Brief pause

23. 1

Pause 3 seconds

24. Feel yourself becoming very relaxed

Pause 3 seconds

25. Put your attention on your breath as it travels through your body.

Pause 3 seconds

26. Focus on the sensations that you experience as you breathe in and out.

Pause 3 seconds

27. Feel the weight of your body as you go deeper and deeper into relaxation.

Pause 3 seconds

28. As you relax, you will experience thoughts, emotions, and perceptions

Pause 3 seconds

29. These are natural phenomena that are part of your existence.

Pause 3 seconds

30. You are about to explore the nature of emotions. Any realizations that you make regarding your emotions can be applied to your thoughts and perceptions.

Pause 3 seconds

31. Notice what you are feeling right now.

32. If you are unable to identify the emotion, that is okay. Developing a deeper understanding of emotions does not require you to have the correct term for them.

33. Just ask yourself what the emotion feels like. Does it feel negative, neutral, or positive?

Pause 3 seconds

34. Treat the emotion you are experiencing as though it was a rare bird, and you are the bird watcher.

Pause 3 seconds

35. The bird watcher does not intrude upon the bird or alter its behavior.

Pause 3 seconds

36. Similarly, do not try to change, control, or resist any emotion you experience.

Pause 3 seconds

37. To observe an emotion is to be aware of its existence.

Pause 3 seconds

38. You are about to be asked a series of questions about what you are experiencing.

39. When answering these questions, do not resort to logic or your imagination. Instead, go by your direct experience.

Pause 3 seconds

40. What can you observe about the emotion that you are experiencing?

41. Does it have a color?

Pause 3 seconds

42. Does it have a size?

Pause 3 seconds

43. Does it have a shape?

Pause 3 seconds

44. Where is it located?

Pause 3 seconds

45. Is the emotion you are experiencing confined to a specific space, or is it without boundaries?

Pause 3 seconds

46. Is the emotion you are experiencing fixed and permanent, or is it continuously changing in its level of intensity?

Pause 3 seconds

47. As you observe the emotion, is it causing any problems for you?

Pause 3 seconds

48. Take another deep breath. Hold it.

Pause 5 seconds

49. Slowly let it out.

Pause 3 seconds

50. Breathe normally, and relax.

Pause 3 seconds

51. Now think of a time in the past when you experienced this emotion.

Pause 5 seconds

52. Recall the situation as vividly as you can.

Pause 5 seconds

53. Can you determine what triggered its appearance?

Pause 3 seconds

54. How did experiencing this emotion then differ from what you are experiencing now?

Pause 3 seconds

55. If you feel less impacted than you did in the past, it is because you are aware of the emotion without engaging with it.

Pause 3 seconds

56. You got curious about it rather than getting caught up on it.

Pause 3 seconds

57. Now say to yourself, "My emotions have no power over me unless I allow them to." When you say it, say it with meaning. Do it now.

Pause 3 seconds

58. Now say again, "My emotions have no power over me unless I allow them to." When you say it, say it with conviction. Do it now.

Pause 3 seconds

59. Emotions possess no power of their own. You give emotions their power by getting caught up in them.

Pause 3 seconds

60. Accept whatever emotion enters your awareness.

Pause 3 seconds

61. Observe them with curiosity without losing yourself in them.

Pause 3 seconds

62. You will now hear a count from 1 to 5.

63. With each count, you will become more awake.

1... Feel yourself beginning to awake.

2... Experience your mind becoming more active.

3...Feel your body becoming more energized.

4... Move your hands, feet, and neck.

5... Open your eyes and feel refreshed.

Pause 3 seconds

64. Take as long as you want to savor your experience before getting up.

Emotions are a natural aspect of who we are. Further, there are no good or bad emotions. It is we who give meaning to emotions. Learn to accept all of your emotions as you would accept a guest. When you accept your so-called negative emotions, they will lose their power over you. Practice this meditation daily until you can do this.

Guided Meditation for Transforming your Emotions

In this meditation, you will transform a negative emotion into a positive or neutral one. This meditation will require that you stay present while experiencing negative emotions.

1. Sit down in a comfortable position and close your eyes.

2. Follow your breath during inhalation and exhalation. Focus on your breath; feel it as it courses through your body.

3. Now think about a situation that concerns you. As you think of this situation, observe the emotions and sensations that arise from within you.

4. Now ask yourself, "What does this situation mean to me?" As you respond to this question, pay attention to the feelings that you are experiencing.

5. Now ask yourself, "What I am experiencing, what does it feel like?" For example, you may be experiencing tension. Using this example, the next question you would ask yourself would be, "What does tension feel like?" Continuing with the example, I would say that tension feels constricted and heavy.

6. Notice that the question was not what you think about tension; do not involve your thoughts in this process. Ask yourself, "What does it FEEL like?" Get in touch with what your experience FEELS like. Also, do not doubt yourself; go with the first answer that comes to you. Do not worry about your words; focus on identifying the feeling. Make sure that you continue to breathe as you experience the feeling. Allow yourself to dive into it.

7. Whatever your response was to the last question, ask yourself, "What does that feel like?" Going back to the previous example, if

tension feels like my body is constricted and heavy, the next question I would ask myself is, "What does be constricted and heavy feel like?" Continuing with my example, I would say, "Being constricted and heavy feels like I am being crushed by a boulder." Whatever answer you receive, get in touch with its feeling. Making sure that you continue to breathe as you experience the feeling.

8. Whatever your response was to the last question, ask yourself, "What does that feel like?" If my response were that being constricted and heavy feels like I am being crushed by a boulder, I would then ask myself, "What does be crushed by a boulder feel like?"

9. The format for this exercise is to repeatedly ask yourself, "What does it feel like?" After asking the question, dive into the feeling and fully experience it. As always, continue to breathe.

10. When you continuously ask these questions and allow yourself to experience the feelings fully, the feeling will transform on its own.

11. You will know when you reach the end when the previously unpleasant feeling is now pleasant or neutral.

12. You can also use this same meditation on positive emotions, in which case, the positive feeling of the emotion will expand.

13. Repeat this exercise until you can successfully transform a negative emotion. Just for clarification, emotions are not positive or negative; they feel negative or positive by the meaning we give them. This is why this meditation works; you are giving your emotions attention without imposing judgment on them.

The last exercise was intended to transform negative emotions. In the next exercise, you will learn how to harness positive emotions. This exercise can be used to experience any positive emotion that you desire. In explaining this exercise, the emotion of happiness is used.

1. Get in a comfortable position and relax.

2. Close your eyes, take a deep breath, and then let it out slowly.

3. Now think of a time when you were the happiest.

4. Now go back to that memory when you were the happiest.

5. Where were you at that time?

6. Make your memory as clear and detailed as possible as you think of that place.

7. As you think about that time, notice how you feel.

8. Focus on the feeling and try to intensify it. When you reach peak intensity, say to yourself your favorite color or number.

9. Now go back to that memory again. What were you doing at that time that made you happy?

10. Make your memory as clear and detailed as possible as you reflect on what you were doing.

11. As you think about what you were doing, notice how you feel.

12. Focus on the feeling and try to intensify it. When you reach peak intensity, say to yourself your favorite color or number.

13. Now go back to that memory again. Who was around you when you did that thing that made you happy?

14. Make your memory as clear and detailed as possible as you think back to who was around you.

15. As you think about that time, notice how you feel.

16. Focus on the feeling and try to intensify it. When you reach peak intensity, say to yourself your favorite color or number.

17. Now go back to that memory again. When you were doing that thing that made you happy, what did you see?

18. Make your memory as clear and detailed as possible as you think back to what you saw.

19. As you think about that time, notice how you feel.

20. Focus on the feeling and try to intensify it. When you reach peak intensity, say to yourself your favorite color or number.

21. Now go back to that memory again. What did you hear when you were doing that thing that made you happy?

22. Make your memory as clear and detailed as possible as you think back to what you heard.

23. As you think about that time, notice how you feel.

24. Focus on the feeling and try to intensify it. When you reach peak intensity, say to yourself your favorite color or number.

25. Now go back to that memory again. Did you taste or smell something when you were doing something that made you happy?

26. If so, make your memory as clear and detailed as possible as you reflect on what you smelled or tasted.

27. As you think about that time, notice how you feel.

28. Focus on the feeling and try to intensify it. When you reach peak intensity, say to yourself your favorite color or number.

29. Now open your eyes. Say to yourself your favorite color or number. Do you feel a change in how you feel? Keep practicing this exercise until saying your favorite color or number brings about your desired emotion.

Practice these last two meditations until you experience their transformative powers. Keep practicing; it will be worth it! You will harness the emotions you desire and reduce the potency of those emotions you do not want to experience.

Guided Visualization

An insecure attachment style is like a bad habit when it no longer serves us. One way to change your habits is to go straight to the subconscious level through visualization. When first learning how to tie your shoes or drive a car, odds are that you were not very good at it. Learning to do these things took a lot of concentration and practice. The more you practiced doing these things, the more effective you became. There came a point when you did not even have to think about how to do these things because they were ingrained in your subconscious.

When changing a habit, you need to replace it with a new one and practice it over and over. However, rehearsing the new behavior does not have to occur exclusively in the real world. You can also rehearse the new behaviors in your mind. By visualizing in your mind the new behaviors that you want to adopt, you can speed up the time that it takes for them to become part of your life.

Visualizing is simple if you keep this in mind: everyone visualizes differently. While some people see vivid images, others see murky ones. Both of these are fine. When visualizing, trust whatever it is that you are experiencing.

1. Think of a minor change that you would like to make. You want to start small. Using visualization, you can deal with the bigger changes when you become more experienced.

2. When you have identified the change that you wish to make, get into a relaxed state. You can focus on your breath, or meditate.

3. When you are relaxed, visualize yourself in a situation where you want to change your behavior. For example, if you want to be more assertive, visualize yourself in a situation where you want to express how you feel. Make your visualizations as detailed as you can.

4. Imagine yourself being how you want to be. If you want to be more assertive, see yourself becoming more assertive.

5. As you visualize yourself being how you want to be, incorporate your five senses. When you are being assertive, what do you see? What do you feel when you are being this new you? Do you hear anything? Do you sound differently when you speak? Do you smell or taste anything?

Practice visualization twice a day for a few minutes. Also, bolster your visualization practice with real world practice. You can do that by committing to a plan. For example, you will practice being assertive anytime you feel a need to express yourself.

Guided Meditations for Relationships

Healthy relationships begin with partners that are emotionally aware of themselves. They also seek to be emotionally supportive of their partners. The following guided meditations address these points.

Guided Meditation for Healing Your Relationships with Others

No relationship is free from upsets or disagreements. When this happens, it is easy for our emotions to take charge and make things worse. The following meditation provides a way to begin to heal relationship wounds.

1. Sit down in a comfortable position and close your eyes.

    Pause 3 seconds

2. Now breathe deeply, hold your breath briefly, then exhale.

    Pause 3 seconds

3. Feel the relaxation in your body.

    Pause 3 seconds

4. Feel yourself becoming more and more relaxed.

    Pause 3 seconds

5. Follow your breath during inhalation and exhalation. Place your attention on your breath. Feel it as it courses through your body.

    Pause 3 seconds

6. You are about to be asked to recall a memory. Know that you are safe and protected. When you recall the memory, imagine that it is a movie and that you are watching it from the audience.

    Pause 3 seconds

7. I want you to think of someone you believe treated you unfairly or unjustly. It can be recent or from the past. When you have this

person in mind, I want you to relive the specific situation where this person mistreated you.

Pause 3 seconds

8. Where did the situation take place?

Pause 5 seconds

9. What were the surroundings like? What did you see?

Pause 5 seconds

10. Where was this person when the situation happened?

Pause 5 seconds

11. What were they doing at the time?

Pause 5 seconds

12. See it in your mind; visualize it in as much detail as possible.

Pause 10 seconds

13. Where were you at the time?

Pause 3 seconds

14. What were you doing when the situation happened?

Pause 3 seconds

15. What did they say or do to you that caused you to be angry or hurt?

Pause 3 seconds

16. How did you feel when it happened?

Pause 3 seconds

17. What did you tell yourself?

Pause 3 seconds

18. Now breathe deeply, hold your breath briefly, then exhale.

Pause 3 seconds

19. Feel the relaxation in your body.

Pause 3 seconds

20. Feel yourself becoming more and more relaxed.

Pause 3 seconds

21. Follow your breath during inhalation and exhalation. Place your attention on your breath. Feel it as it courses through your body.

Pause 3 seconds

22. Feel yourself getting more and more relaxed.

Pause 3 seconds

23. I want you to replay the situation in your mind a second time. This time I want you to observe this person without judgment. Observe the situation objectively.

Pause 3 seconds

24. Where did the situation take place?

Pause 5 seconds

25. What were the surroundings like? What did you see?

Pause 5 seconds

26. Where was this person when the situation happened?

Pause 5 seconds

27. What were they doing at the time?

Pause 5 seconds

28. See it in your mind; visualize it in as much detail as possible.

Pause 10 seconds

29. Where were you at the time? What were you doing when the situation happened?

Pause 3 seconds

30. What did they say or do to you that caused you to be angry or hurt?

Pause 3 seconds

31. Now ask yourself: "Am I 100% positive that this person intended to hurt me?"

Pause 5 seconds

32. Also, ask yourself: "Is there any chance I misinterpreted the situation?"

Pause 3 seconds

33. Ask yourself: "Is it possible that I am projecting my thoughts and emotions on this person?"

Pause 5 seconds

34. Now ask yourself this question: "This thing that I am accusing this person of, is it possible that I am doing the same thing to myself by holding on to these emotions?

Pause 5 seconds

35. If this is true for you, ask yourself, "How can I be more loving toward myself?"

Pause 5 seconds

36. Now breathe deeply, hold your breath briefly, then exhale.

Pause 3 seconds

37. Feel the relaxation in your body.

Pause 3 seconds

38. Feel yourself becoming more and more relaxed.

Pause 3 seconds

39. Follow your breath during inhalation and exhalation. Place your attention on your breath.

Pause 3 seconds

40. We can only behave at the level of awareness that we are at. If we were at higher levels of awareness, we would make different choices. Now say to yourself: "I am healing my relationships through compassion for myself and others." When you say it, say it with meaning. Say it now.

Pause 5 seconds

41. Say it again, with even more conviction: "I am healing my relationships through compassion for myself and others." Experience what you feel when you say this. Say it now.

Pause 5 seconds

42. One last time, say it with the meaning: "I am healing my relationships through compassion for myself and others." Experience what you feel when you say this. Say it now.

Pause 5 seconds

43. Now breathe deeply, hold your breath briefly, then exhale.

Pause 3 seconds

44. Feel the relaxation in your body.

Pause 3 seconds

45. Feel yourself becoming more and more relaxed.

Pause 3 seconds

46. We attract into our lives that which matches our intentions. However, our intentions need to be pure and based on the desire that everyone involved benefits.

Pause 3 seconds

47. The statement "I am healing my relationships through compassion for myself and others" is an intention. Our intentions can manifest into reality when we release our intention while experiencing a quiet mind.

Pause 2 seconds

48. Now breathe normally. As you breathe, place your attention on your breath. Notice the sensations you experience as your breath travels into and out of your body.

Pause 3 seconds

49. Feel yourself becoming more and more relaxed. Enjoy the feeling.

Pause 2 seconds

50. Continue to follow your breath as it enters and leaves your body.

Pause 2 seconds

51. Feel yourself becoming more and more relaxed.

Pause 2 seconds

52. Accept everything that enters your awareness without any judgment.

Pause 2 seconds

53. Become more and more relaxed.

Pause 2 seconds

54. Feel yourself going deeper and deeper within. Allow yourself to surrender to everything that you experience.

Pause 5 seconds

55. Continue to breathe and remain aware of the flow of your breath.

Pause 2 seconds

56. Now make the intention: "I am healing my relationships through compassion for myself and others." Do not hold on to this intention. As soon as you are aware of it, let it go. Release your intention to the universe.

Pause 2 seconds

57. By letting go, you allow the universe to organize the situations and events that will support you in making your intention a reality.

Pause 5 seconds

58. I will guide you in coming out of your meditative state. When you awake, know that you will be guided by life toward achieving your intention each day. Treat each experience as a teacher who is there to point the way.

I will now count to five. With each count, you will come closer to exiting your meditative state:

1. Feel yourself beginning to awake.

2. Experience your mind becoming more active.

3. Feel your body becoming more energized.

4. Move your hands, feet, and neck.

5. Open your eyes and feel refreshed.

6. This is the end of this exercise.

Guided Meditation for Relationship Success

1. Sit down in a comfortable position and close your eyes.

   Pause 3 seconds

2. Now breathe deeply, hold your breath briefly, then exhale.

   Pause 3 seconds

3. Feel the relaxation in your body.

   Pause 3 seconds

4. Feel yourself becoming more and more relaxed.

   Pause 3 seconds

5. Follow your breath during inhalation and exhalation. Place your attention on your breath. Feel it as it courses through your body.

   Pause 3 seconds.

6. I want you to visualize the person that you want a relationship with. In your mind, see their face and hear their voice.

Pause 5 seconds.

7. As you think about this person, notice any feelings that may appear.

Pause 5 seconds.

8. Now imagine yourself talking to this person. See yourself being confident and relaxed as you talk to them.

Pause 3 seconds.

9. See yourself and this person enjoying each other's company. Also, see yourself not having any expectations as you converse with them. Just enjoy the moment.

Pause 3 seconds.

10. Now imagine that you and this person are on a date. You are dining in a restaurant and have your private booth. You have an enjoyable conversation. As you get to know this person, what are some of their needs? What are they looking for?

Pause 5 seconds.

11. What can they offer you? What needs of yours can they meet?

Pause 5 seconds

12. Now ask yourself what you can offer this person. What can you give to them?

Pause 5 seconds

13. Now breathe deeply, hold your breath briefly, then exhale.

Pause 3 seconds

14. Feel the relaxation in your body.

Pause 3 seconds

15. The exchange that you just experienced occurred in your mind. Though this is obvious, what is less evident is that everything we experience originates from the mind.

Pause 2 seconds

16. Everything we see, hear, smell, taste, and touch is an interpretation our brain makes. Our senses take in information from the environment and convert it into electrical impulses. Our brains interpret this information. When we have an experience, we experience an interpretation that we created.

Pause 2 seconds

17. Your brain cannot distinguish between an actual date or you imagining one. Everything that you experience in this meditation is a projection of your mind.

Pause 2 seconds

18. Relationship success comes from learning to accept yourself, including your perceived flaws fully.

Pause 2 seconds

19. You are perfect just the way you are. It is when we have a lack of self-acceptance that we create resistance within ourselves. It is this resistance that prevents us from experiencing relationship success.

Pause 3 seconds

20. Now breathe deeply, hold your breath briefly, then exhale.

Pause 3 seconds

21. Feel the relaxation in your body.

Pause 3 seconds

22. Feel yourself becoming more and more relaxed.

Pause 5 seconds

23. Now say to yourself: "I fully accept myself as I am."

Pause 3 seconds

24. Say it again, with even more conviction: "I fully accept myself as I am."

Pause 3 seconds

25. Experience what you feel when you say this.

Pause 5 seconds

26. One last time, say it with meaning: "I fully accept myself as I am." Experience what you feel when you say this.

Pause 3 seconds

27. Now breathe normally. As you breathe, place your attention on your breath. Notice the sensations you experience as your breath travels into and out of your body.

Pause 3 seconds

28. Feel yourself becoming more and more relaxed.

Pause 3 seconds

29. Accept everything that enters your awareness without any judgment.

Pause 2 seconds

30. Become more and more relaxed.

Pause 2 seconds

31. Feel yourself going deeper and deeper within. Allow yourself to surrender to everything that you experience.

Pause 5 seconds

32. Continue to breathe and remain aware of the flow of your breath.

Pause 2 seconds

33. Now make the intention "I fully accept myself as I am."

Pause 2 seconds

34. Do not hold on to this intention. As soon as you are aware of it, let it go. Release your intention to the universe.

Pause 2 seconds

35. By letting go, you allow the universe to organize the situations and events that will support you in making your intention a reality.

Pause 5 seconds

36. I will guide you in coming out of your meditative state. When you awake, know that you will be guided by life toward achieving your intention each day. Treat each experience as a teacher who is there to point the way.

Pause 2 seconds

37. I will now count to five. With each count, you will come closer to exiting your meditative state:

1... Feel yourself beginning to awake.

2… Experience your mind becoming more active.

3…Feel your body becoming more energized.

4… Move your hands, feet, and neck.

5… Open your eyes and feel refreshed.

This is the end of this exercise. In the next section, we will explore the use of affirmations.

Affirmations

As with guided meditation, affirmations can also be a useful tool for creating a more secure attachment style.

How Affirmations Work

Affirmations are empowering statements we make to ourselves with a sense of conviction. By repeating affirmations, one creates a new focal point for attention. The increased attention leads to the affirmation becoming established in one's belief system.

Each time you repeat an affirmation, you strengthen your beliefs about what is true. You are also strengthening your vision of what your life can become. The reason for this is that repeating affirmations rewires your brain.

When you first start repeating affirmations, it may seem like you are just going through the motions. You may feel that nothing much is happening, that you are just repeating words.

If this is your experience, do not be disappointed, as this is normal. Repeat your affirmations as often as you like. The more you repeat them, the more ingrained they will become in your consciousness.

It takes about a month of consistently repeating affirmations before you notice any changes. One of the changes you will notice is that the affirmation will replace your limiting beliefs. Your mind will become conditioned through empowering thoughts. If a negative thought appears, your affirmation will automatically take its place.

How to Use Affirmations

To be effective, affirmations need to be experienced emotionally. Many people make the mistake of simply repeating the affirmation to themselves, which has little power. To be effective, affirmations need to be accompanied by emotional intensity. When you repeat an affirmation to yourself, say it like you mean it!

For this reason, you must choose an affirmation that you believe in. You need to believe what you are saying. If you do not believe in the affirmation, you will just be repeating words.

When reciting affirmations, you may feel a sense of calm or relief. If that is the case, you have selected an affirmation that is right for you. The following are suggestions for using affirmations:

- Choose affirmations that resonate with you. You want to select affirmations that are meaningful to you. You also want to choose an affirmation that matches the outcome you want to achieve.

- Affirmations work better when you can hear yourself speak the words. Say your affirmation out loud while standing before a mirror. Do this for five minutes, three times a day.

- You can also write out your affirmations in your journal. Writing them out or saying them aloud is superior to just thinking about them. When writing your affirmations, focus on one affirmation at a time. As with reciting your affirmation, the more you write it out, the better.

- Visualize your affirmations as though you were experiencing them in your current reality.

When visualizing, see yourself thinking and behaving consistently with your affirmation.

The following are the affirmations.

- My life is a gift for me to discover and unwrap.

- I am loved by the universe, and all of my experiences are for my pruning.

- I proudly express my beliefs and what I stand for.

- I am strong and nurturing.

- I am proud and beautiful.

- I am not a stereotype; I am a person.

- My dignity and worth as a human being are granted by my creator.

- I deserve to be here.

- I deserve the chance to make a difference in my world.

- I deserve to take up space to create a better life for myself.

- I am worthy of respect.

- I am worthy of an opportunity.

- I am intelligent and wise.

Affirmations

- I am liberating myself from the chains of my negativity.

- I am intelligent and capable.

- I am worthy because I exist.

- I am strengthened by my love for others and myself.

- I am loved. I give love. I am in love.

- I deserve all the good things that come to me.

- I take responsibility for my health.

- I take time for self-care because I am worth it.

- I take care of myself so that I can do God's work.

- I honor myself by being true to who I am.

- I have something to give to this world.

- I have something to contribute to the making of a better world.

- I celebrate life for giving me life.

- I stand up for life, for life is sacred.

- I embrace the abundance that life has to offer.

- I am a good person, and I am worthy.

- I am a source of love, strength, and faith.

- I honor and believe in myself.

- I have something to offer the world.

- I am grateful to be born into life.

- My happiness is deserved because I exist.

- I am growing as a person

- I deserve a place at the table.

- I deserve to be part of the conversation.

- I am more than enough to be successful.

- I am good enough just being me.

- I will honor my pain.

- I affirm the need to acknowledge my pain.

- I am embracing freedom, for it is my divine right.

- I validate my feelings because they are my connection to my soul.

- I am worthy of all good things in life.

- My life matters, for it, comes from the source of life itself.

- I am worthy of respect and dignity.

- I am worthy of appreciation.

- I love myself for who I am.

- I am a light of God.

- I forgive others.

- I am worthy of success.

Affirmations

- I am determined to be successful.

- I am committed to achieving my dreams.

- I forgive myself.

- I am committed to my success.

- I am blessed with love.

- I am blessed with faith and hope.

- I embrace love.

- I celebrate my life and the life of others.

- I am the manifestation of love.

- I am worthy of being cherished.

- How I feel is a decision that I make.

- I forgive the past and embrace the future.

- I love me.

- I love myself.

- I cherish who I am.

- I value my health.

- I am in control of my mind.

- I love myself.

- I love the way I look.

- I take care of my health, for it is a gift from my creator.

- I am powerful.

- I love living healthfully.

- I take care of myself emotionally and physically.

- I am where I am supposed to be at this moment. It is my starting point for greatness.

- I add value to this world.

- My body is healing itself of illness.

- I am creating a legacy for my loved ones.

- I take care of myself because I am worth it.

- I love challenging myself.

- I give and embrace love.

- I am breaking through the bondage of lies that I was told.

- I am passionate about living healthfully.

- I am blessed to be alive.

- I am becoming stronger and wiser.

- I am in charge of my health.

- I am focused and disciplined.

- My love and wisdom run deep.

- I am blessed with good fortune.

- I am blessed with love.

- I am becoming healthier and stronger.

- I am the captain of my destiny.

- I respect myself, and I respect life.

- I love myself and my life.

- My life is radiant; like a precious jewel, it shines.

- I am blessed with hidden talents.

- In the art of life, I am a masterpiece.

- I have everything that I need

- I am prosperous in heart and spirit.

- I am proud of who I am.

- I have boundaries because I respect myself and others.

- I am open to life.

- What I think matters.

- What I have to say matters.

- I determine how I define myself.

- I seek help because we are all connected and support each other.

- I love myself just the way I am.

- I am grateful for all of my life's experiences.

- I believe in myself because I am an expression of my creator.

- I am valuable because I have something to give.

- I am in tune with myself.

- I practice self-care.

- I am a great person because of who I am.

- I am adventurous and fun-loving.

- I am a proud and beautiful woman.

- I love being me.

- I am worthy; I deserve all good things that come to me.

- I am loved, and I love.

- I am compassionate and caring.

- I do not have to explain or justify who I am. I am worthy of respect just the way I am.

- I choose to be happy and successful.

- I have no need to impress others or to prove myself. I am worthy of happiness for just being me.

- I accept and love myself for who I am.

- I take time for myself because I deserve it.

- I am worthy of happiness.

- Today, I will believe in myself.

Affirmations

- I am worthy of all my desires.

- I love my hair texture. It is beautiful. It is me.

- I set boundaries for myself out of respect for myself.

- I spend time centering myself.

- I set boundaries out of respect for myself and others.

- I am a loving and supportive friend.

- I am healthy, strong, and beautiful.

- I strive for only the best for myself and others.

- I am a loving soul, and I am loved by others.

- My strength is in my vulnerability.

- I can love others because I love myself.

- I do not have to do anything to prove my self-worth.

- I belong where ever I am.

- I always win when I am myself.

- I am loved and supported by the universe.

- My worth as a woman is beyond measure.

- My self-worth is without conditions.

- I am gentle and caring with myself throughout life's changes.

- I honor my feelings, for they are valid.

- I heal myself by allowing myself to experience all that I feel.

- My gifts and individuality speak for themselves.

- I refuse to hold on to shame, for it does not serve me.

- I come closer to healing whenever I embrace my inner child.

- I will achieve my dream life by taking full responsibility for my life.

- I honor myself by taking care of myself.

- I take care of myself because I have compassion for myself.

- I take care of myself so that I can take care of others.

- I commit myself to self-care because I deserve it.

- I take play seriously because it is restorative to my life.

- I use my body in ways that bring me joy.

- I prioritize rest, for it is what keeps me going.

- By being intentional, I exert less energy but accomplish more.

- I turn my attention to my breath when life gets too busy.

- My having fun is as important as my work.

- I do not have to know other people's business to remain informed.

- I give my peace of mind the highest priority.

- My greatest treasures are peace, stillness, and simplicity.

Affirmations

- My inner calm repels chaos.

- I care for myself so that I can care for others.

- I am beautiful and worthy of happiness.

- I am beautiful in my own right, as are others.

- I am worthy because my life has dignity.

- Each day, I give to myself and my business.

- I deserve to take care of myself because I work hard.

- I embrace my flaws as areas of opportunity for growth.

- I honor my hopes and dreams.

- I have the right to say "no."

- I allow myself to say "no," without guilt.

- I take my time to do things correctly instead of taking shortcuts.

- I am grateful for the mind and body that I was given.

- I do not give up on myself.

- I speak my truth and uphold my dignity.

- I stand tall and take pride in myself for being who I am.

- I am learning to forgive myself and others.

- I am a human being, and I demand that I be treated as such.

- My value as a person is self-evident and immeasurable.

- I do not allow others or society to define my self-worth. My self-worth is unlimited.

- My opinion matters, and I have self-worth.

- I am worthy of respect and of giving respect.

- I deserve abundance in my life.

- I believe in myself and do not give in to the opinions of others.

- I am nurtured by the love that I have for others and myself.

- My life is rich because I deserve it.

- I take care of myself. It is my responsibility to myself and my loved ones.

- I treat self-care as being as important as caring for others.

- My body is God's temple. Self-care is my expression of appreciation.

- I learn to appreciate myself more and more with each day.

- It is in my acknowledging my pain that I begin the process of my healing

- My life and freedom are the same, and they are my divine right.

- I love and embrace myself just as I am.

- I love myself just as I am.

- I let go of guilt and embrace forgiveness for myself and others.

- Forgiveness is the healing water that washes away the residue of my guilt.

- I free myself from the shackles of guilt and shame and rise on the wings of forgiveness.

- When I embrace love, I embrace myself.

- I am the manifestation of the love that created me.

- I love myself for being me.

- I have love and compassion for myself.

- My uniqueness is the spice of my humanity.

- I care for my health because I deserve a happy life.

- I love myself unconditionally.

- I engage in self-care so that I can offer more of myself.

- I am loved because I give love.

- I am living a healthy lifestyle and feeling better about myself.

- I practice self-care because I am worth it.

- My self-worth is without limits.

- I take pride in myself.

- I celebrate my life.

- I make my health and well-being a priority.

- Being focused and disciplined is my expression of self-love.

- When I am self-disciplined, I am demonstrating self-love.

- I treat my physical well-being as a priority.

- I set boundaries out of love for myself and my respect for others.

- I, and I alone, determine how I want to be and live.

- I reach out for help when needed, for we are here to support each other.

- I love the person that I am.

- I take care of myself without guilt.

- I am a great person for being honest with whom I am.

- I love the way that I am.

- I love being who I am.

- I am worthy of all blessings that have entered my life.

- I am loved, and I love.

- I am engaged in self-care to offer value to others and myself.

- I am proud, and I do not have to justify myself for being me.

- I exhibit grace and dignity.

- I am radiant and living.

- I am happy and successful, just as I am.

- I honor my past.

- My existence matters.

- I feel no pressure to be anyone other than me.

- I embrace myself for being the person I am.

- I take care of myself because I am worth it.

- My life matters.

- I deserve happiness.

- My worthiness is beyond what I even can imagine.

- My personal happiness is more important than the expectations of others.

- My happiness is as important as anyone else's.

- How I feel matters.

- I adore how I look.

- My dreams are being realized.

- I celebrate my small victories.

- I have faith in the person who I am.

- I am deserving of all that I have received.

- I conduct myself to a higher standard.

- I am compassionate and understanding with myself.

- My body is a beautiful work of creation.

- I establish boundaries for myself as part of self-love.

- I take time to go within and experience silence.

- I am grateful for being the person I am.

- I honor myself for all that I sacrificed.

- My boundaries provide a safety zone for me.

- My boundaries let others know how I expect to be treated.

- My boundaries help me form healthier relationships.

- I respect the boundaries of others as I do my own.

- I am proud of the woman that I am becoming.

- I have compassion for others because I have compassion for myself.

- I do not have to do anything to prove my worthiness.

- I belong here.

- I always win when I am being myself.

- I am good enough, just as I am.

- Who I am is becoming more with each day?

- Each day, I discover more about myself.

- My self-worth is unconditional.

- What I am feeling is valid, and it is part of my reality.

- I allow all of my feelings to present themselves without getting caught up in any of them.

- I am constantly growing and improving myself as a person.

- I let my feelings and energy guide me in life.

Affirmations

- I do not allow others to define me.

- The only person that I compare myself to is myself.

- I align myself to my life by trusting what feels right for me.

- I am deserving of self-care and self-love.

- I nurture myself so that I can nurture others.

- I honor my life, for it was bestowed on me for a reason.

- My life rejuvenates and restores itself when I give it attention.

- My body is beautiful and scared.

- I take care of myself because I am worth it.

- I am intentional in the way that I live.

- My privacy and alone time are sacred.

- I seek peace and simplicity.

- My growth and happiness are my responsibility.

- I am beneath no one, nor am I above anyone.

- I care for myself so that I can care for others.

- I am beautiful just as I am.

- I am beautiful and worthy of happiness.

- I am beautiful in my own right, as are others.

- I choose to be happy.

- I am whole; I have everything that I need to feel complete.

- I belong, and I have something to bring to the table

- I love my skin color.

- I love my hair.

- I honor my hopes and dreams.

- I make decisions that come from a place of love and caring.

- I have the right to say "no."

- I can say "no," without feeling guilty.

- I take my time to do things correctly instead of taking shortcuts.

- I do not feel self-pity, for I am a gift to others and myself.

- I love who I am, and I appreciate who I am.

- I do not need others to feel complete. I am complete as a person and enjoy and value my solitude.

- My past has no control over me.

- I love who I am, and I do not judge or criticize myself.

- I am happy being with me; I am comfortable in my own skin.

- Life loves me, and I love life.

- I am not beholden to anyone to warrant me sacrificing my happiness.

- I am learning to trust my decisions because I am learning to trust myself.

- I honor my body, for it is my temple to my creator.

- My mind and body were shaped and sculpted by my creator. My creator's hands carefully molded me to carry on his glorious work.

- I will not tolerate being judged for my skin color.

- I am growing as a person, and I have faith in my process.

- I will no longer compare myself to others.

- I celebrate my progress in becoming a better person.

- Every step forward that I take is deserving of my acknowledgment.

- I strive to always improve myself, yet, I will never reach perfection.

- I am ever-evolving in my knowledge, wisdom, and beauty.

- I have unconditional love for myself.

- I will not tolerate suggestions from others or myself that I am less than others.

- I do not need anyone's permission to do what I feel is right for me

- I am creative with great ideas.

- My presence in this world is meaningful as I make a difference simply by being me.

- My presence in this world is meaningful because I can make a difference.

- My presence in this world is meaningful because I care.

- I love my abilities and talents.

- I am patient with myself and give myself room to learn and grow.

- All the qualities I need to be happy and successful lie within me.

- I am good enough, capable enough, and worthy enough to succeed.

- I have intrinsic worth.

- I deserve the best, for I am worthy.

- Though others may not believe in asking for help, I do. It is my choice, and I deserve it.

- Though my family may not believe in seeking help for mental health concerns, I do. I deserve to be happy.

- My family may not believe in seeking help for health concerns, but I do. It is my choice, and it is my body.

- I am deserving of well-being, inner peace, and love. I deserve to be prosperous. I do not associate with anyone that believes otherwise.

- I look back to remind myself of all I had to overcome to be here today. In doing so, I celebrate my strength, determination, and resiliency.

- I speak from the heart.

- I am learning to love and appreciate myself.

- My compassion for others is growing.

- I have complete acceptance of my strengths and my weaknesses.

- I feel balanced and secure in my life.

- I remain centered as my emotions drift by like clouds.

- If I feel anxious around others, it is because I am receiving the message that I have forgotten the glory of who I am.

- Overcoming self-doubt takes time. I am loving and patient with myself, and I keep moving forward.

- I accept myself for who I am because that is the way to victory.

- Like the wings of a newly emerged butterfly, my flaws become my wings when they are brought to the sunlight of my acceptance.

- I am dragging my self-image out of the shadows of my judgments and presenting it to the light of self-love.

- I am worthy just as I as I am.

- I am enough because my creator made me who I am.

- My self-confidence is growing.

- I am confidently and courageously pursuing my dreams.

- I am complete as I am, and I am good enough.

- I am worthy of my boldest dreams, and I am worthy of manifesting them.

- I trust in my ability to succeed, and I believe in myself.

- Within me lies the power and great strength, and I am learning to express it.

- I do not let others' opinions of me shake my sense of dignity and self-worth.

- I accept that others may have opinions that clash with mine.

- I do not engage in spreading gossip or untruths about others.

- I am no less and no more deserving of good things than others.

- I am good enough and worthy enough.

- I am. Enough said.

- I accept that prejudice and sexism exist, but I will not hold on to hate or resentment.

- I provide support to others in a way that is consistent with my self-respect and dignity.

- I embrace my gifts, talents, and strengths.

- I can offer new perspectives and ideas that reflect my experience.

- I will use the perceptions that others have of me to empower me. I will never let the perceptions of others make me feel less.

- I let go of the need to impress others, for I have nothing to prove. I am perfect just as I am.

- I honor my need for rest and relaxation. I will honor myself by taking time daily for "me time."

- I love the way that I look. I love all of my features, including my imperfections.

- I offer value to people. I am a valuable resource for them.

- I enjoy showing others who I am and what I can offer.

- I take time for myself to relax and have a break. I treat self-care as a priority.

- I love myself, and I treat myself with respect. For this reason, I do not take on more than I can handle.

- I am comfortable saying "no" when it is necessary. My time is valuable, and I deserve to spend it as I choose.

- I bring a unique perspective to the table and my unique background.

- I am greeted by my creator's love every morning, and I am renewed.

- The strength and love of my creator reside within me at every moment.

- I am confident and strong.

- I am filled with the love and energy of the universe, and it renews me.

- I am proud of who I am.

- I am a gentle soul.

- I am a force for good.

- My feelings count.

- My life matters.

- I honor my feelings.

- I honor my beliefs.

- I am intelligent and wise.

- I am worthy of being where I am.

- I deserve everything that I have attained.

- I deserve to take care of myself because I work hard.

- I am good enough just as I am, yet, I strive to improve each day.

- I embrace my sexuality.

- I am forgiving and accepting of myself, and I move forward with my life.

- I am like a masterpiece. I am a classical work of art.

- I have no need to impress others as I have nothing to prove. I fully accept myself.

- I do not compare myself to others; I only judge myself by how far I have come in becoming a better version of myself.

- I am a strong and resilient woman.

- I choose to feel happy. I have the power to do so, and I have the right.

- I do not allow anyone in my life to disturb my sense of emotional well-being. I will replace them with those with who I share a connection.

- I affirm my humanity and allow myself to experience all of my emotions, make mistakes, fail, and succeed.

- I let go of my guilt, resentments, and hurts and opened myself to healing.

Final Words

One of the most important things to understand about attachment styles is that they are not some mental illness or disorder. They are learned ways of thinking and behaving, and we all have one. We can think of attachment styles as a language. We all grew up learning a certain language. Unless we have a secure attachment style, the language we grew up with no longer serves us.

We need to learn a new language to live a happier and more fulfilling life.

Using language as a metaphor for attachment styles is also valuable for my next point. Who you are as a person is not defined by the language you speak. Similarly, your attachment style does not define who you are either. You are not your attachment style. Rather, your attachment style shapes how you think and behave within certain moments of your relationships. I hope this book motivates you to make the necessary changes so that you may live the life you deserve.

Book #2

Avoidant Attachment Recovery

Break Free from Avoidant Habits to Build Secure
and Long Term Relationships

Introduction

Have you ever entered a relationship where the other person seems uncomfortable with emotional closeness? Maybe you have experienced this yourself. You want to get close to your partner but cannot get yourself to do it. Just the thought of it makes you feel anxious.

I remember my relationship with men when I was younger. I wanted to be in a relationship, yet I always held back. I rarely initiated anything in my relationships, and I felt like leaving whenever I felt emotionally vulnerable. It was only years later that I learned that I had an avoidance attachment style.

If you ever wondered why the person you are with seems to keep their distance, it may have nothing to do with you. If you are the one who is having trouble getting close, I can reassure you that it is not your fault. I am saying this because the organizing principle behind this avoidance is subconscious, and its roots may have begun in childhood.

Attachment styles influence how we relate to others, especially in intimate relationships. These attachment styles were forged when we were infants and shaped by our relationship with our parents or caregivers. There are three major attachment styles, one of which is the avoidance attachment style. This attachment style leads to fear and mistrust of emotional intimacy. Though attachment styles are formed when we are very young, they often carry over to adulthood.

Though I have a strong background in psychology, I was unaware of the details of attachment styles until later in my life. As I studied attachment theory, I began to understand why I, and the people in my past, behaved the way they did. The experience of learning about attachment styles was very illuminating for me for these reasons, which is why I decided to write this book. I wanted to share this information with others. Though there are numerous other books on attachment styles on the market, I felt compelled to write this book because I know what it is like to have avoidant tendencies.

In this book, you find information about how the avoidant attachment style develops, how it impacts us, what it does to our relationships, and how you can move beyond the fears associated with it. As the avoidant attachment style does not exist in a vacuum, you will also find out about the other attachment styles and how they interact with the avoidant style. Whether you have an avoidant attachment style, or your partner does, this book can shed light on a relationship challenge that often leads to misunderstandings and hurt feelings. When there is light, there is an opportunity for growth and healing.

CHAPTER 1

What is an Attachment Style

When I was younger, I felt very insecure with men. Though I wanted to be in an intimate relationship, it scared me. I was afraid they would find out who the real me was and that I would be rejected. Because of this, I tried to keep things at the surface level. I did not show vulnerability and avoided getting involved in emotional encounters.

Though I was successful in keeping emotionally distant from my partners, I was never successful in my relationships. Because of my behavior, my relationships never lasted long. Most of them ended in less than a year. When my relationships ended, I always blamed myself. I felt that I was cursed. I wanted to be loved, but I was afraid of getting hurt. This created a vicious cycle. My lack of success in my relationships only reinforced my fears of being vulnerable.

Sometime later, I had to relocate to another state for work reasons. I did not know anyone except for my new co-workers. If I was not working, I would spend most of my time alone in my apartment. Though I have always spent my time alone, being alone this time was different.

My new environment caused me to reflect on my life. I began to realize that I was unhappy with how my life was going. I made the decision to see a counselor about my fears of becoming vulnerable with others. It was through therapy that I learned that I had an anxious attachment style. To understand what an anxious attachment style is, you first need to understand attachment theory.

In the 1930's psychologist, Harry Harlow did an experiment that helped pave the way to understanding attachment theory. I do need to point out that I find Harlow's experiment unethical, but it did provide insight into attachment styles.

In the experiment, Harlow took infant rhesus monkeys and separated them from their mothers. He then constructed two surrogate mothers. The first surrogate was constructed out of metal and had an artificial nipple from which the infant monkey could nurse. The second surrogate was made of a soft and fluffy material but did not provide nourishment.

When hungry, the baby monkeys went to the first surrogate. However, they went to the second one when they wanted comfort, as the second surrogate gave them a sense of security. When the baby monkeys were with the second surrogate, they were curious and explored their surroundings. When they encountered something, they were unsure of, they returned to the second surrogate.

When the infant monkeys were put in a new environment, without the second surrogate, they would not explore. Instead, they rocked back and forth on the floor and sucked on their thumb. Harlow's experiment demonstrated that the baby monkeys' need for comfort was just as important as nourishment. The second surrogate allowed the infant monkeys to build trust and confidence.

Harlow's experiment led to further study, including that of psychoanalyst John Bowlby. In 1969, Bowlby wrote his theory of human attachments. He believed that attachments were an instinctive emotional connection that made possible the exchange of care, comfort, and pleasure among individuals.

From an evolutionary perspective, Bowlby believed that attachments made it possible for the survival of our species. It was the attachment between mother and child that kept babies close to their mothers, thus, ensuring their survival. Bowlby identified four characteristics of attachments that make the relationship between parent and child meaningful:

Closeness: We desire to be near the person we have an attachment to.

Safety: The object of our attachment makes us feel safe.

Comfort: The comfort we get from our attachment figure gives us the confidence to explore our surroundings.

Separation Anxiety: We are anxious when our attachment figure is not around.

In the 1970s, Mary Ainsworth expanded Bowlby's studies by conducting her landmark study, the Strange Situation experiment. (Edward, 2017). In the experiment, Ainsworth investigated how children between 12-18 months responded when their mothers left them alone for brief periods.

In the experiment, a mother and her child were placed in a room alone. Ainsworth observed how willing the child was to explore while their mother was present. Later on in the experiment, a stranger would enter the room and briefly talk to the mother. The mother then would briefly leave the room, leaving the stranger with the child.

Based on her observations, Ainsworth created the three major attachment styles: Secure attachment, anxious attachment, and avoidant attachment.

The Attachment Styles

From the moment of our birth, we form attachments with our primary caregiver. These attachments became fully formed around the age of three.

The quality of the attachment that we formed with our primary caregiver determined our ability to trust others. As with the infant monkeys, having our emotional needs met allowed us to develop confidence, trust others, and explore the unfamiliar. However, if our emotional needs were not met, we did not develop the ability to trust others or explore the unknown.

Research has identified four different styles of attachments:

- Secure attachments

- Anxious attachments

- Avoidant attachments

If we had our emotional needs met as a child, we formed a secure attachment with our primary caregiver. We learned to trust others and build confidence within ourselves. The remaining attachment styles are based on fear, as our emotional needs were not met. They lead to anxiousness and mistrust of others. For this reason, they are known collectively as insecure attachment styles.

The attachment style that we developed as children may follow us into adulthood, which is knowing your attachment style can clarify your relationship challenges. The following is a brief explanation of the four attachment styles:

- **Secure Attachment Style:** You feel confident and recognize your self-worth. You can be open and supportive toward your partner.

- **Anxious Attachment Style:** You lack trust in your relationship and doubt your partner's feelings for you. As a result, you need constant reassurance from them.

- **Avoidant Attachment Style:** You fear becoming emotionally vulnerable and distance yourself in the relationship when there are feelings of emotional intimacy.

In the United States, an estimated 56% of the population has a secure attachment style, followed by 20% for the anxious style, 23% for the avoidant style, and 1% for disorganized (Hazen and Shaver, 1987). In the next chapter, we will take a deeper look at how attachment styles are created.

Note: The disorganized style will not be addressed in this book because of its rarity.

CHAPTER 2

How Did You Develop Your Attachment Style?

The previous chapter offered a brief explanation of how attachment styles are formed. In this chapter, we will take a deeper look into this. Attachments are lasting emotional connections between individuals. Through these connections, individuals seek security and closeness.

In adult-child relationships, attachments are developed by how the adult responds to the child's needs. Additionally, the attachment to the adult by the child is not based on the adult that spends the most time with them but rather by the adult that most meets the child's needs. The meeting of the child's need for a sense of security is the essence of attachment theory. The child needs to be able to find security when they feel threatened or unsure.

In the early 21st century, the National Research Council and the Institute of Medicine's Committee on Integrating the Science of Early Childhood Development came to the following conclusion:

"Children grow and thrive in the context of close and dependable relationships that provide love and nurturance, security, responsive interaction, and encouragement for exploration. Development is disrupted without at least one such relationship, and the consequences can be severe and long-lasting." Their conclusion would shape their policies and practices. (Cassidy, Jones, and Shaver, 2013).

The Power of Connection

The fundamental premise of attachment theory is that a child's fears are lessened when they are in proximity to the person with whom they have formed an attachment. What creates trust in the child is the child's perception of the availability of that person to comfort them and make them feel safe. It is this perception that allows the child to determine if they can handle a perceived threat. If they feel they can handle a perceived threat, they will feel less anxiety and fear.

Even at a very early age, infants can take in complex information about the social interactions they observe. The information that is being referred to is both social and emotional in nature. In other words, infants can determine if the interactions that they witness are caring or adversarial.

Studies were done where puppets were used to demonstrate either supportive or adversarial relationships. The infants that observed the puppets were able to identify the kind of relationship the puppets had with each other. The infants showed a preference for those puppets that were supportive toward others. The researchers concluded that the infants knew what type of relationship the puppets should have with each other (Cassidy, Jones, and Shaver, 2013).

Knowing that they have someone who they can depend on for security not only benefits children emotionally, but it may also benefit them at a physiological level, which was demonstrated in a 1970s experiment. The experiment showed that there was a physiological response in infant rats when they were separated from their mothers. The rat pups demonstrated multiple changes in their physiological and behavioral levels. Body temperature, heart rate, food intake, and willingness to explore were all affected.

However, not all the rat pups responded in the same way. Rat pups that received the most attention from their mothers (in the form of maternal licking and grooming) were the least affected when separated. These pups also explored more than the other pups. Additionally, these differences were maintained into adulthood (Cassidy, Jones, and Shaver, 2013).

Attachment research conducted in 1996 showed that toddlers with an anxious attachment style had elevated cortical levels, a stress hormone, when introduced to new situations. The rise in cortical levels was also seen when mothers stopped interacting emotionally with their children. This change in cortical levels was also seen in children from violent homes, even when they were not directly exposed to the violence (Cassidy, Jones, and Shaver, 2013).

All evidence from the research points to the same thing. For healthy development, children need a caregiver that provides them with a sense of security, and they need to feel that they can depend on receiving that security when needed.

Internal Working Model of Attachment: Inside the Mind of an Infant

From the time they are born, children experience their primary caregivers. It is from these experiences that they form a mental representation of their relationship with them. In attachment theory, these mental representations are known as internal working models of attachment (IWM). IWM influences how children interact and form relationships with others. The child's expectations when interacting and forming relationships with others are based on their IWM.

A child's IWM is like a GPS or internal guidance system. It lays down the path for how the child will respond emotionally and behaviorally when interacting with others. This pathway can last throughout the child's lifetime unless there is a conscious decision to change.

The challenge is that these IWM operate beyond our conscious awareness, which is why changing them is difficult though possible. If not consciously addressed by the person, or there are no intervening events in the person's life, their IWM will remain operative throughout their lives. This is the reason why the quality of the parent-child relationship in the early stages of life is a strong predictor of the child's relationships when they become adults. Unless there is some form of intervention, IWMs can become intergenerational. Children with an avoidant attachment style are more likely to pass on this attachment style to their own kids when they become parents.

The Stages of Attachment Development

Bowlby identified four stages in the development of attachments, pre-attachment, attachment in the making, clear-cut attachment, and goal corrected.

The pre-attachment stage occurs between birth and two months. During this stage, the infant shows interest and is responsive to interactions with anyone they encounter. They have not yet developed an attachment to any single individual. Because of this, they are not stressed if a loving and responsive caregiver takes over as the primary caregiver. What is important to the infant is that the person can comfort them.

Attachment-in-the-Making

This second stage occurs between the ages of two and six months. The infant starts to develop a preference for an individual caregiver. They express this through smiling and vocalizing. This is also the stage when infants become anxious when they encounter someone they do not know.

At this stage, the baby does not only develop an attachment with its primary caregiver but with others as well. This is also the stage when babies start to explore. While investigating their world, they keep an eye on their primary caregiver. It is the presence of the primary caregiver that gives the baby the confidence to explore.

Clear—Cut Attachment

This stage occurs between the ages of six months and two years and is marked by the child developing a strong attachment to their primary caregiver. They show signs of distress if separated from the primary caregiver for more than a brief period. In cases of prolonged separation, children may develop major trauma.

At this stage, the child's attachment to others is deeply ingrained. The child has created IWMs of its relationships. As the child gets older, this internal model becomes more and more difficult to change. As our IWMs operate subconsciously, they become our experience of reality. We are unaware that our relationship issues are due to our attachment styles.

Goal-Corrected Partnership

This fourth stage occurs from age three to adolescence. This is the stage when the child's need to be with their primary caregiver becomes progressively less, given that the child knows where their caregiver is and their availability to them. This is also the stage when children learn that other people are separate individuals with their own personalities, thoughts, and desires.

At this phase, there is a transformation in the child's attachment relationships. The child's understanding of relationships changes from focusing on getting their needs met to the formation of reciprocal relationships. This is the stage where the child uses language to express their needs and is aware of space and time.

This is also the stage when children can benefit by engaging with others (other than the caregivers) regularly, as in the case of preschool. How children respond to their relationships with others will be shaped by the quality of attachments they form in the earlier stages.

What Shapes a Child's Attachment?

While there are stages to the development of attachments, there are also two factors that determine how a child's attachments will develop. Those two factors are quality and critical period.

Quality

Research shows a child's primary attachment figure is not based on how much time a person spends with the child but rather on the quality of the time that the person provides them. The primary attachment is the strongest form of connection for the child. However, the child also forms secondary attachments with those other than the primary attachment figures.

These additional attachments, also known as subsidiary attachments, vary in their level of intensity. A baby can form stronger attachments with people other than the primary caregiver if others provide a greater quality experience than the primary caregiver.

Critical Period

The critical period is the period when a child's early attachments are formed. During this time, the brain's plasticity is receptive to the influence of the attachment experience. When this period passes, the child's attachment pattern becomes deeply ingrained and is difficult to change.

Theories on Attachment Formation

So far in this chapter, you have learned about what attachments are, the stages of their formation, and the factors that shape them. But how are attachments formed? There are two theories regarding this, learning theory and evolutionary.

Learning Theory

Under the learning theory, all of our behaviors are learned as opposed to being innate or instinctual. Namely, a child is born as a blank slate. The child learns different behaviors through conditioning and association.

When a baby is fed by their mother, the baby learns to associate the mother with food. Conditioning can also be involved in behavior. The child learns that by engaging in a specific behavior, the child gets rewarded. An example of this is when a baby smiles, and their mother smiles back or kisses them.

Because the behavior (smiling) led to a favorable outcome, the baby will repeat this behavior in the future. Conversely, if the baby engages in a specific behavior that leads to a negative outcome, it will avoid repeating that behavior in the future.

Evolutionary Theory

While learning theory is based on the idea that our attachments to others come about through the process of learning, the evolutionary theory states that our attachments are hardwired within us from birth. Both Bowlby and Harlow (McLeod, 2017) believed that we are born preprogrammed to form attachments to others for survival purposes.

Under this theory, infants are born with the means to connect with others. These means come in the form of smiling, crying, and other behaviors that elicit nurturing responses from adults.

Based on this theory, attachments need to be formed within the first five years. If an attachment is not made within this period, the child will develop irreversible consequences to its development, such as increased aggression and reduced intelligence (McLeod, 2017). In the next chapter, we will take a deeper look into the different attachment styles. Though this book is about the avoidant attachment style, it is important to understand the other styles to create context.

CHAPTER 3

How to Determine Your Attachment Style

Before going into greater detail about the different attachment styles, read the following statements and see if any of them resonate with how you feel about yourself:

- "It is easy for me to connect with others. In my relationship with my partner, I have no problem depending on them. Also, I have no problem with them depending on me."

- "I am not happy with the level of emotional intimacy in my relationship. My partner is not as close to me as I would like them to be. Also, I often have doubts if they really love me."

- "I am not comfortable getting emotionally close to others, nor do I feel comfortable when they try to get close to me."

The first statement you read is what a person with a secure attachment may think. The second statement exemplifies the thinking of someone with an anxious attachment style, and the third statement reflects the thinking of someone with an avoidant attachment style. What follows is a more detailed look at each of the three styles.

Secure Attachment Style

Those with a secure attachment style tend to have healthy and long-lasting relationships. This attachment style was born out of a secure relationship with one's caregiver. In this kind of relationship, the child can freely express their need for validation or reassurance without fearing negative consequences.

In Ainsworth's experiment, she found that children who had a secure attachment exhibited the following:

- They were comfortable exploring the room while their mother was there.

- They went to their mother for comfort when they felt unsure.

- They greeted their mother with positive emotions when she returned to the room.

- They preferred being with their mother over a stranger.

The key to a secure attachment style is that the caregiver makes the child feel understood, valued, and safe. This is made possible because their caregiver is emotionally available for them. Additionally, the caregiver is self-aware. They are aware of their own emotions and behavior. The child learns from the caregiver and models their behaviors. Signs that you have a secure attachment style include:

- You can regulate your emotions.

- You readily trust others.

- You can communicate effectively.

- You can ask for emotional support.

- You are comfortable being alone.

- You are comfortable in close relationships.

- You can self-reflect on your relationships.

- You connect easily with others.

- You can manage conflicts.

- You have good self-esteem.

- You are emotionally available.

When you carry a secure relationship style into adulthood, you feel emotionally secure and can navigate relationships in a healthy way. You are also trusting, loving, and emotionally supportive toward your partners.

Anxious Attachment Style

Children develop an anxious attachment style when they learn that they cannot depend on their caregivers to meet their emotional needs. This attachment style comes from inconsistent parenting and not being attuned to the child's needs.

In this kind of child-parent relationship, the child does not feel a sense of security with their caregiver. The inconsistent parenting creates confusion for the child. In Ainsworth's experiment, children with this attachment style showed a high degree of distress when the mother left the room.

Inconsistent parenting is not the only way anxious attachment styles can form. This attachment style can also come from experiencing traumatic events or when parents are overly protective of a child. In this case, the child picks up on their parent's insecurity, which makes them fearful.

Those with an anxious attachment style may have had parents who:

- Were not consistent in comforting their child. Sometimes they may have comforted the child, while at other times, they were indifferent or detached.

- Were easily overwhelmed.

- Alternated between being attentive toward their child and pushing them away.

- Made their child feel responsible for how they felt, which may lead to the child becoming codependent later in life. The child grows up believing that they are responsible for other people's feelings (PscyhCentral).

Signs that you may have an anxious attachment style include:

- You are codependent.

- You have a strong fear of rejection.

- You depend on your partner for validation.

- You have clingy tendencies.

- You are overly sensitive to criticism.

- You have a need for validation from others.

- You have a problem with jealousy.

- You have difficulty being alone.

- You have low self-esteem.

- You feel unworthy of love.

- You have a strong fear of abandonment.

- You have issues with trust.

In relationships, your anxious attachment style may show up in the following ways:

- You feel unworthy of being loved and need continuous validation from your partner.

- You believe that they are responsible for the challenges in the relationship.

- You can become intensely jealous.

- Your low self-esteem causes you to distrust your partner.

- You are overly sensitive to your partner's behaviors and emotions. As a result, you jump to conclusions about your partner's intent.

These signs come from a strong fear of abandonment. Though you may want an intimate relationship, your fear of abandonment keeps you from developing the relationship you desire. Also, those with this attachment style may focus on their partner's needs at the expense of their own.

This attachment style can also develop in adulthood. This may occur if someone experiences inconsistent behavior from their partner. If a partner is inconsistent in expressing affection, or if they are emotionally abusive to them, the other person may develop anxiety or insecurity about the relationship. This often occurs in abusive relationships.

In an abusive relationship, a partner may constantly tell them that they are incompetent or stupid. Eventually, they may believe it. Because of this, they may cling to their partner. They rely on their partner to care for them because they do not believe that they can do it on their own.

Avoidant Attachment Style

The avoidant attachment style is formed when the caregiver of the child is strict, emotionally unavailable, or absent. The child does not feel supported, and they feel that they have been left to fend for themselves. Those who have an avoidant attachment style have difficulty forming long-term relationships as they fear emotional and physical intimacy.

As children, these individuals may have experienced the following:

- There was an expectation that they be independent before they were ready to be.

- They were punished for depending on their caregivers.

- They were rejected by their caregivers when they expressed their emotions or needs.

- Their basic needs were not a priority.

This kind of parenting does not always come from outright neglect. It may be that the parent was overwhelmed with other responsibilities. Regardless, the child grows up to be strongly independent and is uncomfortable looking toward others for support.

You may have an avoidant attachment style if you:

- You have a pattern of avoiding emotional or physical intimacy.

- You are fiercely independent.

- You avoid expressing your feelings.

- You have a dismissive attitude toward others.

- You cannot trust others.

- You feel anxious when others try to get close to you.

- You avoid interacting with others.

- You believe that you do not need others.

- You have commitment issues.

When they are in a relationship, individuals with this attachment style keep their distance; thus, there is a lack of emotional intimacy. The partners of those who have an avoidant attachment often feel like they do not know them and often feel stone-walled. In Ainsworth's experiment, children with the avoidant attachment style did not show a preference between their mother and the stranger. Also, they did not seek out comfort from their parent.

Important Note

Most people will not be an exact match for the profiles just described. The attachment styles cover a spectrum, so these profiles would only fit the most extreme cases. Normally, a person will show a mixture of attachment styles.

Attachment styles can only be determined by a trained professional. The purpose of this book is not to diagnose but rather to recognize unhealthy behaviors that may be interfering in your relationships so that you can address them.

Also, the attachment styles described are not intended to predict children's future behavior. Nor should it be inferred that our caregivers are responsible for our relationship challenges as adults. A child may begin life with anxious attachments but change for the better when they get older or vice versa.

There are numerous experiences that we have as we grow into adulthood that can influence our attachment styles. However, the attachment styles that we form as children can help predict our behavior later in life. Research shows that the best predictor of our attachment style as adults is the way we perceive our relationship with our parents and our parents' relationship with each other.

In the remaining chapters, we will explore the avoidant attachment style in greater detail.

CHAPTER 4

Avoidant Attachment Style

It is natural for us to crave love and affection and with good reason. From an evolutionary perspective, emotional intimacy is important for our development and growth, regardless of our age. Emotional intimacy allows us to share our thoughts and feelings with others. By connecting with others, we can support and reassure each other. Emotional intimacy allows us to feel recognized, valued, and appreciated. All these things help us feel emotionally safe.

Though they cannot articulate it, infants have a need for emotional intimacy. In fact, it is at this age that the foundation of emotional trust is forged. In their own way, the infant can determine whether they can trust and depend on their caregiver.

As with all attachment styles, the emotional availability of the caregiver is the determining factor for which attachment style the child will develop. The avoidant attachment style is created when the caregiver is largely emotionally unavailable to the child. The caregiver is not attuned to the child's emotional needs.

The child learns that the caregiver is not responsive to their needs. The caregiver has not responded to the child's cues, and the child gives up on getting the caregiver's attention. When the child does express emotions, it may elicit anger from the caregiver. Instead of expressing compassion and caring, the caregiver may become angry with the child because they want the child to become independent before it is age appropriate. As the child grows older, they adopt behaviors that allow them to meet their needs without connecting with others.

Caregivers who are likely to create an avoidant attachment in children are likely to be uncomfortable with displaying emotions, whether those emotions are positive or negative.

They may be physically present but devoid of the emotions to address the child's needs. The caregiver may be reserved and back off when the child seeks affection, support, or reassurance. It is not uncommon for such caregivers to have been raised by parents who treated them the same way.

From the time we are born, we are hardwired to desire emotional closeness. It is natural for the child to want to bond with the caregiver. After being persistently rejected by the caregiver, the child realizes they must go without the affection and attention they so profoundly desire. As a result, the child will suppress their need for emotional closeness and comfort. Psychology professor and distinguished scholar Jude Cassidy writes:

"During many frustrating and painful interactions with rejecting attachment figures, they have learned that acknowledging and displaying distress leads to rejection or punishment." By not crying or outwardly expressing their feelings, they are often able to partially gratify at least one of their attachment needs, which is remaining physically close to a parent" (Catlett, 2022). These children learn they will not be comforted; they give up seeking closeness and no longer express their emotions.

As a result of such care giving, the child does not learn how to manage their emotions. They become distrustful of others and avoid emotional intimacy. It is this process that creates the avoidant attachment style. The following are examples of caregiver behaviors that may lead to the development of an avoidant attachment style:

- Ignoring the baby or child when they cry.

- Not expressing emotional reactions to the child's achievements or issues.

- Mocking the child for their concerns.

- Expressing annoyance at the child when they are experiencing problems.

- The avoidance of physical contact or touch.

- When the child is fearful or in distress, the caregiver may separate from the child physically.

- When the child is fearful or distressed, the caregiver becomes irritated with them.

- Shaming the child when they express themselves emotionally.

- Unrealistic expectations for the child to demonstrate independence when it is not age appropriate.

- Telling the child to "grow up," "stop acting like a baby," or "stop your crying" when the child expresses emotions.

- They ignore the child's cues that they are in distress.

Caregivers who are most likely to demonstrate these behaviors include those who:

- They were raised by parents with an avoidant attachment style.

- Are very young or inexperienced. They do not understand how to support their child.

- They have difficulty expressing empathy.

- Have a mental illness.

- Feel overwhelmed by parental demands.

- They are preoccupied with their career or demanding lifestyles.

It should be noted that these behaviors by the caregiver are not always intentional. Some caregivers who engage in such behaviors may want to do what is best for the child, but they do not know how, as their parents were distant from them. A mental illness such as depression can also prevent the caregiver from meeting the child's emotional needs.

Further, children exposed to such behaviors are not guaranteed to develop an avoidant attachment style. Factors such as the infant's unique emotional and behavioral characteristics and temperament may be behind this. Studies also show that some factors beyond caregiving practices can contribute to children developing this attachment style; such factors include traumatic events and life experiences such as a parent's death, divorce, parental illness, and adoption (Catlett, J., 2022).

While emotionally unavailable caregivers can cause the avoidance attachment style, this attachment style can also develop from an emotionally enmeshed environment. In enmeshed homes, there is a lack of personal boundaries and minimal privacy, if any. This kind of environment commonly leads to depression, fear, anxiety, guilt, shame, and grief. These conditions can lead to children having difficulty identifying and expressing their feelings, thus becoming emotionally unavailable (MacWilliam, 2022).

The Two Kinds of Avoidant Attachment Styles

There are two kinds of avoidant attachment styles, fearful and dismissive. These two types differ in how they respond to others.

Fearful-Avoidant vs. Dismissive

Fearful avoidants tend to withdraw from emotional intimacy out of fear, while dismissive avoidants have a disregard for the need to connect with others.

Individuals who have fearful avoidance generally have low self-esteem, along with being very anxious. They do not believe that they are worthy of love. Those with a dismissive avoidant style have a very high level of self-esteem and low levels of anxiety. They have a very positive self-image.

Of the different insecure attachment styles, those with the fearful-avoidant type have greater emotional challenges. They are more likely to experience depression and be less assertive. Also, they may appear to behave in ways that seem confused, aimless, or contradictory when feeling stressed.

Those with a dismissive avoidant style come across as being cold, and they tend to view others in a negative way. They do not feel a need to gain the acceptance of others and view others who seek emotional support as being weak. In fact, they often do not view relationships as being necessary.

Avoidant Attachment Style vs. Avoidant Personality Disorder

Unlike avoidant attachment style, avoidant personality disorder is a personality disorder. We all have personality traits; some of us are shy, while others are extroverts. Being shy is not a disorder because it does not prevent the person from functioning day today, nor is it a significant source of stress.

Having an avoidant personality can be debilitating as it can prevent day-to-day functioning and be a significant source of stress. Avoidant personality disorder is one of the more severe personality disorders, as it can lead to severe social dysfunction. While the avoidant attachment style does not lead to avoidant personality disorder, avoidant personality disorder may be associated with an avoidant attachment style.

Common Characteristics of Avoidant Style Attachment in Children

Children with an avoidant attachment style may exhibit the following characteristics:

- They are resistant to being comforted by their caregivers.

- They seem to be very independent.

- They seem to not desire nurturance or affection.

- While they will seek to be near their caregiver, they avoid having contact with them.

Another characteristic of an avoidant style in children is that they withhold the expression of their distress. In Chapter 2, there was a mention of Ainsworth's "strange situation" experiment. As a reminder, the children with the avoidant attachment style appeared to remain calm when the caregiver left the room. When the caregiver returned, the child avoided contact with them.

From their outward appearance, these children seemed to be calm; however, this is deceiving. When their physiological responses were measured, these children showed the same level of distress as those with secure attachments. Children with an avoidant style suppress their fears (Li, 2022).

Avoidance Attachment Style in Adults

Adults with the avoidance attachment style appear confident, independent, self-directed, and self-assured. They give the appearance of being in control of their lives. Since they avoid emotional intimacy, they often focus on their careers. For this reason, they may be very successful.

They also may have a lot of friends, sexual partners, and acquaintances, and they can be fun to be with. Because they do not seek emotional support, their connections with others remain superficial. The following are signs that an adult may have an avoidance attachment style. They tend to:

- Avoid physical touching and eye contact.

- Do not ask for help.

- May have unusual eating habits.

- Have difficulty sharing their emotions or feelings.

- Accuse their partners of being over-attached or too clingy.

- Do not accept emotional support from others.

- Avoid intimacy out of fear of getting hurt.

- Choose personal independence over relationships.

- Do not allow their partner to rely on them.

- Appear calm in highly emotional situations.

In addition to these signs, adults with this attachment style may use other strategies to manage their emotions and feel safe. These include:

- Choosing not to get closer in a relationship out of fear of rejection.

- Redirecting their gaze from sights that make them uncomfortable.

- Tuning out during conversations about attachment issues.

- Suppressing their memories of negative events that involved their attachment issues. Further, it is common for these individuals to have few memories of their childhood relationships with their parents.

- Placing much of their focus on themselves and their creature comforts.

- Showing a disregard for the interests or feelings of others.

- Because they resist sharing their feelings, their response to conflicts is to become aloof and distant.

Adults with this attachment style tend to have an inflated view of themselves while having a cynical or negative attitude toward others. Their inflated view of themselves is a defensive strategy to protect their sense of self, which is extremely vulnerable and fearful of rejection. At a deep level, these individuals experience low self-esteem and feelings of self-hatred. They will often react with anger when they feel that their false image is being attacked.

The Advantages of Having an Avoidant Attachment Style

Those with an avoidant attachment style miss out on meaningful and fulfilling relationships; however, having this attachment style has its advantages.

Workplace Advantages

A study (Frankenhuis, 2010) theorized that insecure attachment styles (anxious and avoidant) might have an evolutionary significance. These attachment styles comprise 33-50% of the world's population and are most highly concentrated in areas with instability and poverty. The study points out that while these attachment styles cost the individual, they may benefit the group.

According to the theory, those with an avoidant attachment style have the makeup that allows them to respond to threats quickly and independently, thus increasing the chances of survival for the group members. Because of their sensitivity and quick detection of threats, those with anxious attachment styles are specially equipped to detect threats, which also serves the group.

The abilities of those with insecure attachments carry over to the workplace. The study showed that those with an avoidant attachment style serve the workplace with increased productivity while saving resources. Workers with an avoidant attachment style can quickly identify a workplace issue and either resolve it or reduce its impact.

Also, avoidant-style employees require less support from others. They are very independent and confident in their abilities and decision-making. These factors, plus the fact that they do not desire to socialize with others, make them more efficient at work while reducing the demand for resources.

Also, this attachment style is more likely to be success-driven. Their focus is on work rather than a social life, so they frequently achieve greatness in their careers.

Relationships

Though there can be many relationship challenges with this attachment style, these individuals offer the benefit of being less needy or demanding than the other attachment styles. Further, they tend to be more respectful toward others' boundaries. They will also be more respectful toward their partner's freedom.

Those with an avoidant attachment style tend to be very popular and sociable. They are very confident in social situations because emotional closeness is not involved. This is why this attachment type tends to have many friends instead of close relationships.

Additionally, these individuals are a great source of practical advice as they are guided by logic rather than emotion. For this reason, they are very honest. They will tell you what you need to hear instead of what you want to hear.

In the next chapter, we will take a deeper look into how relationships are affected by this attachment style.

CHAPTER 5

How an Avoidant Attachment Style Affects Relationships

Do you have doubts about ever finding that special person with whom you want to share your life with? Maybe you found yourself following a pattern of having relationships with partners who are emotionally unavailable. You may have started to doubt yourself and wondered if there was wrong with you. If this describes you, there may be a deep-seated reason for why you are experiencing this.

Having a romantic relationship with someone who has an avoidant attachment style is anything but easy. Honestly, not many people can make it work, as it can be a very frustrating and unsatisfying experience. Emotional intimacy in a relationship can only happen when both partners are willing to be vulnerable and communicate their thoughts and feelings.

The partner who has an avoidant attachment style tends to perceive relationships as emotionally draining and stressful. This should not be a surprise, as one of the traits of this attachment style is to be fiercely independent.

As a result, they will frequently feel resentful or uncomfortable when their partner turns to them with emotional needs. Those with an avoidant attachment style want to avoid having to navigate emotions. Because they avoid experiencing emotions, they have little self-awareness of what they are feeling. This is why they feel so easily overwhelmed by the emotional needs of others.

When the partner with this attachment style experiences their own negative emotions or they are put in a situation where they must experience the emotions of their partner, their defenses go up. They will distance themselves from their partner, either physically or emotionally. The following are some examples of distancing behaviors:

- If the partners live together, they will isolate themselves in certain areas of the home.

- They will avoid physical closeness, be it holding hands or sex.

- They will not make future commitments.

- They will not say that they love you.

- They will not listen to or validate their partner's feelings.

- They will walk ahead or behind their partner.

- They will dismiss their partner's feelings, including legitimate frustrations.

- They may engage in addictive behaviors such as sex, gambling, substance abuse, or pornography.

The partner of the avoidant personality is likely to feel confused as they cannot understand them, which leaves them not knowing what to do or think. One of the reasons why partners feel so confused is that the avoidant attachment style, and other insecure attachment styles, have not been covered as widely by the media. Unlike other disorders, such as narcissism, this attachment style has not received nearly as much attention.

If information on this and other insecure attachment styles were more widely available, it would help clear up the confusion of their partners. When this occurs, partners would realize that their partner's behavior is not the result of anything they did. Rather it is part of their partner's emotional dysfunction.

The defense mechanism of this attachment style is to avoid emotional intimacy with their partner, particularly when they are feeling stressed. If the thinking of the avoidant attachment personality could be summed up in one line, it would be: "We coexist, but you do you, and I will do me." The best partner for this attachment style is a person who is satisfied with being in a romantic relationship without much emotional intimacy.

If you are very independent, do not desire much communication or emotional sharing, and are content with your present circumstances, then you might find this kind of relationship satisfying.

As children, the bonding experience that we had with our caregivers was our first relationship. That relationship influenced how we related to intimacy later in life. The three attachment styles can provide insight into not only our behavior but our partner's. Understanding this can help us understand our needs and how to handle the challenges we experience. This is particularly true if a person who has an avoidant attachment style enters a relationship with someone who has an anxious attachment style.

When Avoidant and Anxious Meet

At an unconscious level, we may select partners that respond to us as our caregivers did. Further, how we behave in intimate relationships may be governed by our expectations, which originated from our childhood experiences. In other words, our attachments can cause us to behave toward our partners in the same way we act toward our caregivers.

Are you attracted to someone who may have an avoidant attachment style? If you do, you may consider doing some self-reflection as it may indicate that you have an anxious attachment style. Generally, we end up in relationships with those who validate our pre-existing beliefs regarding relationships.

The outcome is predictable when an anxious style gets into a relationship with an avoidant style. When the avoidant style is stressed, they will distance themselves from their partner. By distancing themselves, the avoidant partner can gain the independence and autonomy needed to regulate their emotions and deal with their distress.

The challenge is that the anxious style partner feels rejected and threatened by feelings of abandonment. In response, they strive to regain their connection with their partner. As their partner is of the avoidance type, they feel even more threatened.

Anxious Attachment Style

The person with an anxious attachment style may be clingy in their relationships; they have a continuous need for attention and love. They also may feel emotionally drained by their ongoing concern about whether their partner really loves them. Other characteristics of the anxious attachment style include:

- You desire closeness and intimacy with your partner, but you are held back by your lack of trust that they will be there for you.

- Your intimate relationship is all-consuming, and it is your primary focus.

- You lack boundaries for yourself and often violate your partner's boundaries.

- Your partner's wish for space threatens you. It may cause you to experience fear, panic, or anger. These feelings only reinforce your fear that your partner is no longer interested in you.

- Your self-esteem is determined by how you feel your partner is treating you.

- You jump to conclusions or overact when you perceive a threat to the relationship.

- You feel anxious when you are not with your partner. Also, you may become controlling or try to make them feel guilty as a way to keep them close to you.

- You seek constant reassurance from your partner.

- Friends or family may tell you that you are clingy or needy.

Those with this attachment style follow a predictable relationship pattern. The early stages of the relationship are marked by excitement and anticipation of what the relationship could become. There is that first kiss and the anticipation for when they can be with the other person. This stage is common in many relationships, and it has an almost addictive quality as there is a release of dopamine.

With time, the relationship begins to level out. This stage of the relationship is also normal, but it is threatening to the person with an anxious attachment style. This person may start to wonder if their partner has lost interest in them.

This sense of doubt puts their partner in a losing position. Even if their partner tries to reassure them, the person with this style of attachment will never be satisfied. They will continue to believe that their partner is losing interest in them. They may have thoughts like:

- Why does my partner not desire me the way that I desire them?

- Why have they not called me? I have not heard from them all day.

- I need to be more attentive to them, and then they will desire me more.

Unlike the authentic bond enjoyed by those with a secure attachment, those with an anxious attachment try to fulfill a bond that is built on a fantasy. Instead of experiencing genuine love, their bond is based on an emotional hunger. They are looking for a partner to rescue them from their own feelings of inadequacy. This usually causes their partner to back away.

Avoidance Attachment Style

Individuals with an avoidance attachment style are fearful of emotional intimacy. For them, freedom and independence are what is most important to them. They feel threatened by intimacy and closeness within a relationship. The following are examples of how this attachment style affects a romantic relationship:

- A person with this attachment style will be very independent and not feel that they need anyone.

- They will pull away if their partner tries to get close to them.

- They are uncomfortable expressing their emotions. If their partner tells them that they are being distant, they will tell their partner that they are being needy.

- They will be dismissive of their partner's feelings.

- They may have affairs as a way to reclaim their sense of freedom.

- They feel more comfortable with temporary or casual relationships than intimate and long-term ones.

- Intellectually, they believe that they do not need intimacy. In their hearts, however, they do desire a close and meaningful relationship.

- They focus on their own needs as they do not feel safe turning to their partner for help. This often leads to a no-win situation, so they do not get their needs met.

The partner with the anxious attachment style craves emotional intimacy but fears it because they are afraid of getting hurt. Further, they do not trust that their partner loves them. The partner with the avoidant attachment style is fearful of emotional intimacy, so they distance themselves. This behavior by the avoidant partner consists of the expectations of the anxious partner. The anxious partner has an expectation that their partner will not be emotionally vulnerable, and the partner with the avoidant attachment style plays this role perfectly.

Attachment Styles and Sex

Attachment styles affect all aspects of the relationship, and that includes sex. When an anxious-styled partner enters a relationship with an avoidant partner, both will be sexually unsatisfied.

Avoidant Attachment Style and Sex

Those with an avoidant attachment style are more likely to engage in casual sex than to develop a loving relationship. This is understandable, given that this attachment style avoids showing emotions. Because of this, they tend to get involved in short-term relationships, engage in casual sex, or not have sex at all.

Instead of intimacy, those with this attachment style are more likely to resort to pornography or emotionless sex. Since sex involves closeness, both physically and psychologically, sex makes them uncomfortable. Rather than being driven by passion and affection, they are sexually driven by their egos. For them, sex is a way to reduce stress, gain status with their peers, or control or manipulate their partners.

Anxious Attachment Style and Sex

Those with an anxious attachment style commonly have an unsatisfactory sex life. This is due to the characteristic behaviors that accompany this attachment style. Individuals with this style excessively worry about what others are thinking about them.

They have a strong fear of being rejected. Additionally, any perceived lack of interest by their partner can cause them to become emotional. Also, they feel misunderstood or not appreciated by their partners. All of this can be a put-off for their partners.

The sexual behavior of those with an anxious attachment style is usually driven by their feeling of a lack of love or security. Because of this, their sexual experiences are unfulfilling. This attachment group is likely to have more sexual partners than other attachment styles. They are also more likely to be unfaithful to their partners. Their motive to engage in sex is often to get their partner's attention, reassurance, and approval.

Avoidant Attachment Style and Work Relationships

Within the last five years, researchers have been paying more attention to how attachment styles play out in the workplace. One study (Hazen and Shaver, 1990) involved the social dynamics of attachment theory in the workplace. Their findings are as follows:

Avoidant Attachment Style in the Workplace

Unsurprisingly, those with an avoidant attachment style have no interest in team building or improving their relationship with their co-workers or managers. In fact, they may have a cynical view of those they work with. These workers have distrust for others and prefer to work alone. The challenge these workers pose to the workplace is that they are not likely to conform to the rest of the group and may be critical and resistant toward their superiors. These are the workers that are most likely to be the troublemakers.

The benefits to the workplace that this attachment style brings are that they tend to respond effectively and without hesitation to workplace threats. Further, they enhance the focus and productivity of their workgroups and are the ones most likely to meet their deadlines (Lavy, Bareli, and Ein-Dor, 2014)

CHAPTER 6

How to Cope with an Avoidant Attachment Style

None of the insecure attachment styles are a form of mental illness. As with the other insecure attachment styles, the avoidant attachment style was adopted during childhood as a way to cope with not getting one's emotional needs met.

The avoidant attachment style served its purpose when it was needed. The challenge is that retaining this adaptation as one grows older poses many challenges. Overcoming an avoidant attachment style involves learning new ways of thinking that support one's happiness and being able to connect with others. Though this may sound simple, making such a change takes patience, determination, and persistence.

Making such a change can be difficult and scary because it requires learning to trust oneself and others, both of which go against the way avoidant attachment styles were programmed. However, it can be done! As healthier ways of viewing oneself sink in, the corresponding behaviors and emotions will follow.

Creating Change

Each of us has the potential to create change in our lives, regardless of age. Though our attachment styles are the result of deep-seated beliefs, we can change them. Creating a change in our beliefs requires that we challenge them. To do so, however, requires support, practice, and patience. The reason for this is our self-talk, our harshest critic, will resist our attempts to change.

This voice was developed from our childhood experience and will do its best to keep us from experiencing our emotions. It is the experiencing of emotions that the insecure attachment styles are designed to save us from.

Fortunately, recognizing one's insecure attachment style is half the battle in creating change. There can be no healing without self-awareness. Understanding one's attachment style lets one know what one must work on. Developing a more secure attachment style is definitely possible regardless of one's insecure attachment style.

Ways to Cope with an Avoidance Attachment Style

There is hope for those with an avoidant attachment style to develop a more secure attachment style within a relationship. However, as with all insecure attachment styles, it is important to clarify that this does not mean that someone with an avoidant attachment style can change into a secure attachment style. Rather, the individual learns to recognize their triggers and respond to them in a more empowering way.

Reflecting on Intimacy

The foundational challenge for the avoidant attachment style is the fear of emotional intimacy. It is here that one's efforts must focus because the switch for turning on intimacy has been on the off position since childhood. Coping with this attachment style involves learning to turn that switch on again. To begin with, you can ask yourself the following questions:

- What emotional and physical sensations do I experience when I think about becoming emotionally intimate with someone?

- What do I need emotionally to feel safe? Answering this question will involve exploring and understanding your needs and the ability to express them to others.

- What can I do to build closer relationships with others? The point behind this question is to create and follow a step-by-step process for allowing others in and dealing with the emotional needs of those close to you.

The following are suggestions for overcoming the avoidant attachment style within an adult relationship:

Face Your Inner Critic

When working to overcome any of the insecure attachment styles, the most challenging opponent you will face is your inner critic, more commonly known as your self-talk. This critical voice was formed in early childhood. Unless we bring our awareness to this voice, we will continue to do its bidding.

It is this inner voice that creates distrust of others, and that warns us that we will be criticized or judged if we express our emotions. Those of us who have an avoidant attachment style use this self-talk to self-regulate our emotions. On the other side of the coin, this voice may be overly protective of us. It may be telling us grandiose thoughts about ourselves to distract us from feelings of lack of self-worth.

To challenge your self-talk, first, spend time identifying the thoughts that you experience regarding emotional intimacy. When you identify these thoughts, challenge them. You can do this by looking for evidence in your life that disproves this thinking. You can then learn to agree to disagree with your self-talk. The following is an example:

You think: "I will not get into a relationship; they will just let me down."

To counter that thought, think of a time when someone in your life was there for you. If you can do this, you will prove your inner critic wrong in this instance.

Honoring Your Need for Personal Space

We all need personal space; however, this is even more true for those with an avoidant attachment style. Having personal space is a must for these individuals as it allows them to ground themselves when stressed, allowing them to feel safer in the relationship.

Know Who to Trust

A major part of overcoming this attachment style is learning to trust others. However, not everyone is trustworthy. For this reason, it is helpful to determine the trust level of those around you. One way to do this is to share with another person some information that is inconsequential to you. If you see that the other person responds respectfully and does not tell others, you will be more likely to trust them with more meaningful information.

Develop Your Communication Skills

For a relationship to be fulfilling and successful, both partners must be open about their thoughts and feelings. For those with this attachment style, sharing their thoughts and feelings is terrifying. For them, it means exposing themselves to potential rejection or criticism. It is also about feeling out of control. For this reason, these individuals must learn to share their feelings in a manner where it feels safe for them, and they are in control.

Both partners must be able to express themselves honestly and openly. By doing this, each partner helps the other regulate their emotions. For this to happen, both partners must strive to communicate clearly to express their concerns without the fear of being judged.

When expressing your thoughts and feelings, pay attention to the physical sensations and thoughts that arise as you do so. In time you will realize that sharing your feelings with others is more enjoyable and healthier than denying them or repressing them.

Imagine that you are talking to your partner, and you sense that it is about to become an argument. It would be normal for an avoidant attachment style to avoid rising emotions by withdrawing from the situation either mentally or physically. Either way, your partner will feel like you are disregarding their concerns.

Instead, here is something that you could say that would honor both of you: "I see things are getting heated right now. Why don't we take a break for a few minutes and continue talking afterward?" If you are in a situation where you need to have some space, you could tell your partner:

- "I appreciate you for always being there for me. I need some space. I promise to discuss your concerns when I am ready."

- "I get how important it is for us to discuss this, but I need time to myself to clear my head. Can we discuss this later? I will be in better shape to talk about it then."

- "We have so much going for us as a couple. Why don't we take a breather and continue this discussion later?"

Therapy

Probably the most effective way to overcome your attachment style is through therapy from a professional who is experienced with working with insecure attachment styles. Studies have demonstrated that therapy can effectively work with avoidant attachment styles (WebMD, 2021).

A good therapist can provide an environment where you can feel safe exploring and expressing your thoughts and feelings. Further, a therapist can help you identify your attachment triggers and how to manage your emotions.

A therapist can help you explore your experiences of the past. By doing so, you will be able to realize what is specifically preventing you from experiencing meaningful relationships and interactions. You can then determine what changes you want and create a plan for accomplishing these changes.

Another reason therapy is so valuable in changing one's attachment style is that it becomes a model for a healthy relationship. It's a safe place to express one's thoughts and feelings. Further, it provides the opportunity to learn new skills for reducing anxiety when talking about topics that are important to you. The following kinds of therapies help deal with avoidant attachment styles in adults:

- Cognitive behavioral therapy (CBT)

- Schema therapy

- Narrative therapy

- Couples therapy

- Psychodynamic therapy

Cognitive Behavioral Therapy (CBT)

CBT is a form of therapy that is effective for treating a variety of issues, including anxiety disorders, depression, eating disorders, and substance abuse. There are numerous scientific studies that demonstrate CBT's effectiveness. CBT differs from many other forms of therapy in that it sees psychological issues as being caused by limited or negative thinking. It also has the following philosophies:

- Psychological issues are based on patterns of behaviors that we learned.

- If you are experiencing psychological issues, you can learn better ways of coping with them, which will lessen symptoms and allow you to become more effective in life.

In CBT, you learn new strategies to:

- Recognize the distorted thinking that is causing your problems and modify your thinking so that it supports you.

- Understand your motivations and the motivations of those around you.

- Learn how to increase your self-confidence in your abilities.

- How to challenge your fears instead of running away from them.

- Learn how to handle difficult interactions through role-play.

- Learn how to relax and calm your mind and body.

Schema Therapy

In psychology, schema is a term for a thought pattern that leads us to engage in unhealthy behaviors or relationship issues. Schemas normally develop in childhood as the result of not getting one's emotional or physical needs met. For this reason, schema therapy is another method for dealing with an avoidant attachment style.

In schema therapy, you will learn to recognize your thought patterns and behaviors that lead to avoidant behavior and learn how to change them. You will also learn more effective ways of coping with relationship challenges. Unlike CBT, there has not been enough research in schema therapy to determine its effectiveness.

Narrative Therapy

Narrative therapy involves realizing the story that you tell yourself, which influences your life. Going through life, you have numerous experiences to which you give meaning. The meaning that you give to these experiences becomes your story. As you go through life, you bring your story with you. This story gives meaning to the experiences you will have in the future and in how you see the world.

A therapist will help you in putting together your narrative. Putting together a narrative allows you to create distance between you and your challenges so that you can see them more clearly.

Narrative Therapy can help with attachment issues, anxiety, depression, grief, and more. Also, there is no judgment, as the client is the expert.

Couples Therapy

Couples therapy is psychotherapy that focuses on helping improve relationships. If you are experiencing relationship challenges, couples therapy can help resolve those issues and rebuild the relationship. Also, couples therapy can be helpful at any stage of a relationship.

If you or your partner has an avoidant attachment style, couples therapy can help you and your partner understand each other better, improve communication skills, and deal with dysfunctional behaviors. The therapist has a range of therapeutic skills, one of which is emotionally focused therapy (EFT). The effectiveness of EFT has been supported by research.

Psychodynamic Therapy

A form of talk therapy, psychodynamic therapy involves talking to a therapist about your challenges, which can lead to feelings of relief and coming up with solutions. Psychodynamic therapy can help you better understand your thoughts, feelings, and motivations.

With a greater realization of your emotional patterns, you will become more effective in problem-solving and or managing your behavior. Psychoanalysis can be used to treat:

- Anxiety

- Depression

- Interpersonal problems

- Social anxiety disorders

- Post-traumatic stress disorder

- Substance abuse

Helping Children with an Avoidant Attachment Style

Helping children with this attachment style takes a two-prong approach. The first approach is directed at the caregiver by offering them education and support. Additionally, family therapy may also be used to help family members communicate more effectively and give them the tools to have more positive interactions with each other. In such cases, the therapy takes place in the person's home.

In the second approach, the therapist works directly with the child with the avoidant attachment style. The therapy aims to help the child develop a sense of self-worth, express their emotions, show empathy, and trust others. The therapy normally involves play therapy and can include puppets, storytelling, and art therapy.

Through such therapy, the child learns to overcome the avoidant attachment style's thoughts, behaviors, and feelings. Ultimately, such therapy is beneficial because it provides the child with a safe environment to try new behaviors and explore their emotions.

CHAPTER 7

Dating and Relationships with a Partner who has an Avoidant Style Attachment

In this chapter, you will find information about dating and relationships with someone who has an avoidant attachment style. We will begin with signs to look out for when dating that may indicate that the other person has an avoidant personality.

Signs that Your Date May Have an Avoidant Style

Imagine that it is your first date and that it is going great. You and your date are enjoying each other's company, and the conversation is flowing. Everything points to the possibility that this may be the beginning of something great.

By the end of the next day, you had not heard from your date. You start getting an uneasy feeling and decide to call them. When you talk to them, they seem distant. When the phone call ends, you are left with nothing to make you feel better about the situation. Before you start thinking that maybe it is something that you did, consider the possibility that your date has an avoidant attachment style.

The following signs may indicate that your date has an avoidant attachment style:

They Do Not Reach Out to You

When you spend time together, they seem to be enjoying themselves, but they never say anything about what it means to them to be with you.

The reason for this is that those with this attachment style want to feel love and connection, but they are afraid to experience these feelings. As a result, they have a compulsive need to distance themselves when they start to experience these feelings. They feel triggered by feelings of emotional intimacy because it leaves them feeling vulnerable to rejection or abandonment.

They Seem Uneasy When You Show Negative Emotions

Those with this attachment style have been conditioned since birth to associate the expression of negative emotions with fear and anxiety. Because they received inconsistent parenting, they have learned that reaching out to others may lead to rejection or abandonment.

You may be expressing negative emotions about something that has nothing to do with your date. However, they may get triggered as though they were the target of your emotions. In other words, they will feel like they are being attacked.

It may seem like they are just not interested in having a serious conversation when, in fact, they are reacting to fear. If you express negative emotions regarding their behavior, they may become defensive as they fear rejection or abandonment at a subconscious level.

They Do Not Ask You for Help or for Favors

Those with an avoidant attachment style are fiercely independent due to their fear of rejection. They are constantly anticipating that they will be disappointed. On the same token, they also do not want anyone looking toward them for help.

Those with this attachment style will often not offer support or help to others when they reach out to them. The reason for this is that they equate offering help or doing favors with making themselves vulnerable. This feeling goes back to when they were being raised and when they were met with rejection when they reached out to their caregivers. If they do a favor for you, they will downplay its meaning. They may even feel irritated if you express your appreciation.

They have Trouble Connecting Emotionally and Communication Difficulties

Research shows that those with this attachment style are less accurate than those with a secure attachment when trying to identify the emotions that others are feeling. When they become stressed, their accuracy becomes even less. As a result, they often misinterpret the behaviors of others or what they say. If your date feels that you are upset when you are not, or they tend to walk away from an argument rather than talking about it, it may be a sign that they have an avoidant attachment style.

They Do Not Communicate Loss

When it comes to loss, be it the death of a loved one or not getting the job they wanted, those with an avoidant attachment style demonstrated the same level of emotions and physiological changes that securely attached individuals do. However, they tended not to verbally express those feelings. Not only did they not verbally express their feelings, but they also suppressed their physiological responses. This was the conclusion of a study by the University of Illinois (Fraley, 2023).

If the person you are dating seems to have a cold or emotionless demeanor after experiencing a loss, it is not because they are resilient. Rather, they have learned to suppress any expressions of vulnerability.

It is for all these reasons that trying to have a relationship with someone who has an avoidant attachment style can be a lonely experience as they will resist allowing the relationship to become meaningful and fulfilling.

When the relationship gets to be serious, they will distance themselves. It is at this point that they will find reasons to break up. This behavior is an expression of how they avoided emotional intimacy with their caregiver.

If someone has an avoidant attachment style, all of these indicators that were just mentioned will be occurring subconsciously. They are reliving their childhood when their caregivers ignored their emotional needs. Their lack of trust in others and the need to care for themselves continues into adulthood. The following is additional information to help better understand them:

Asking for Reassurance

Asking for reassurance from this attachment style may be perceived by them that you are making a huge demand on them. This is because these individuals are extremely vigilant to potential control or manipulation. As children, they learned of the pain that comes from failing their caregivers. After all, why else would their caregivers have distanced themselves from them?

Additionally, they may perceive the request for reassurance as criticism. Finally, avoidant-attached individuals are averse to conflict. They feel threatened discussing any topic that may lead to fighting. Instead, they may behave passive-aggressively and offer you empty promises.

Former Partners

Avoidant attachment styles may maintain contact with ex-partners. They may spend time with them in-person or through social media. Also, they may make their phone off-limits to you. All of this may make you feel like you are their backup plan or that you are competing for their attention.

These individuals use their former partners as a strategy to put you in your place. By doing so, it is hoped that you will feel vulnerable. In turn, your insecurity will make them feel more powerful.

Becoming Their Therapist

Beware of falling for the trap where you give your support to them unconditionally. You may believe that they will become closer to you by doing so. Unfortunately, what usually happens is that it destroys any chance of developing a romantic relationship.

Those with this attachment style treasure friendship over romantic partners. In their minds, the safest way to maintain a relationship with you is to consider you a friend. Though partners with an avoidant attachment style may pull away from the relationship, it does not mean they do not love you.

Avoidant Attachment Style and Triggers

The behaviors of the avoidant attachment style are not demonstrated regularly. As with other attachment styles, the behaviors appear when they are triggered. The dismissive attitude and behaviors that this attachment type engages in are ultimately forms of defense when they feel threatened by separation or loss of a relationship.

When they perceive a threat, some will focus their attention on unrelated issues or their goals. This attachment type will deny their vulnerability, pull away, and attempt to deal with the threat on their own.

When triggered, this attachment type is likely to withdraw and repress their emotions as a way to manage them. At times of crisis, and if they do seek support from their partner, they will be indirect about it. They may resort to sulking, complaining, or hinting.

There are three main triggers that elicit the avoidant behaviors of this attachment style:

- The fear of being taken advantage of.

- The fear of emotional overwhelm.

- The fear of being rejected or abandoned.

The Fear of Being Taken Advantage Of

For those with an avoidance attachment style, maintaining control is of utmost importance. This s one of the reasons why entering a relationship is so scary for them. In their minds, entering a relationship means giving up control. To them, the idea of giving up control to another person means that they would become vulnerable to being exploited or taken advantage of.

Fear of Emotional Overwhelm

For the person with an avoidance attachment style, there is a fear of being overwhelmed by the emotions of another person. They have difficulty managing their own emotions. The idea of taking on the emotions of another is suffocating for them. This is the next reason why individuals with this attachment style retreat from others.

The Fear of Rejection or Abandonment

Many people with insecure attachment styles have suppressed their emotions for years as a way to avoid experiencing their pains. The idea of opening up to another person is very scary for them. Not only would opening up cause them to feel their pain, but they also fear that they will be rejected or abandoned by others. This fear prevents them from forming meaningful connections with others.

Signs that an Avoidant Partner Loves You

It is important to remember that the avoidant behaviors of a person with this attachment style are learned from childhood. They adopted their avoidant behavior for emotional survival. Given this, how can you tell if an avoidant partner loves you? The following are things to look out for:

Nonverbal Signs of Affection

Instead of expressing emotions and affection for their partner, they will demonstrate it in nonverbal ways. These can include affectionate touches, warm smiles, and prolonged eye contact.

Letting Down of Boundaries

As they feel more secure, they may let down their guard and loosen up on their boundaries. It is important to note that relationships go through highs and lows, so they may reestablish their boundaries when there is a down period in the relationship.

Showing Vulnerability

Avoidant partners are uncomfortable with showing vulnerability. If they share their emotions with you, it is a sign that they feel comfortable with you.

Being Responsive to Your Needs

When an avoidant partner is responsive to your needs, it demonstrates that they care about your happiness. When they do so, reinforce them by expressing your appreciation.

Sharing Your Interest

This attachment style has a strong independence streak. If they are willing to get involved with your interests, it may be a sign that they are developing deeper feelings for you.

Wanting to Take it Slow

In a dating relationship, if the avoidant person tells you that they do not want to rush having sex, that is a hopeful sign, as this attachment style tends to be hyper-sexual.

Make Yourself at Home

In the early stages of the relationship, if the avoidant partner leaves you alone in their apartment or home, it is a sign that they trust you. This attachment style is very private, so leaving you in their personal space says a lot.

Going Traveling

This attachment style finds making commitments to be very scary. If they are willing to take a trip with you, that indicates they have serious feelings for you. One word of caution, though, you may want to prepare yourself to be scrutinized by them. They may use the occasion to scrutinize everything you say and do to judge whether there is long-term compatibility.

Willingness to Seek Help

Discussing feelings, being vulnerable, and seeking help are behaviors to which avoidant types have a strong aversion. If your partner is willing to go to therapy, it is a sign that they have strong feelings for you.

Expressions of Endearment

Besides the willingness to seek therapy, another monumental sign that they have strong feelings for you is that they demonstrate acts of service, give you gifts, and engage in physical touch or sex.

Being in A Relationship with Avoidant Partner

If you are in a relationship with someone who has an avoidant attachment style, or you plan to be, there are some important things that you should know so that you can better meet your needs while respecting theirs.

Maintaining a relationship with someone with an avoidant attachment style is very difficult. You will find yourself having to do a balancing act between making your partner feel safe and not compromising your need for intimacy and affection. There are certain rules that you should set for yourself to avoid getting caught up in their attachment style:

Know Your Value as a Person

A big mistake is trying to appease them at your expense. A person with an avoidance attachment style will get bored quickly with those who try to appease them. It is important to know your worth and not turn to them for validation.

Know Your Attachment Style

Because of their unique traits, each of the attachment styles will affect your compatibility with your partner differently. If both partners are of the avoidant style, the compatibility will be high. The partners will respect each other's need for space and discomfort in showing emotions.

A person with an anxious partner is likely to have difficulty understanding the avoidant partner's needs. Understanding your attachment style is invaluable for this reason.

Do not Take it Personally

Regardless of how hard you try to support an avoidant partner; they will need their personal space from time to time. Regardless of how much they value you as a partner, they still need their space.

Set firm Boundaries

Setting boundaries is recommended in any relationship, but it is especially important if you get involved with someone with an avoidant attachment style. You need to know what behaviors you will not tolerate.

Stay True to Your Life

Do not give up on your relationships, hobbies, or interests when getting involved with this attachment style. Of course, this is good advice for any relationship. However, it is especially important for this attachment style. An avoidant partner will dismiss you if you try to pursue a closer connection with them.

Be Clear and Direct

It is important that you are clear, direct, and specific when expressing your needs. If you try to communicate your needs any other way, you will likely get excuses from them.

Do Not Judge

Those with an avoidant attachment easily feel that they are being judged. It is important to them to be able to prove themselves. Avoid saying anything that may sound like you are judging, as that will trigger their attachment style.

Present Them with a Challenge

This is not to imply that you should play games with them. Instead, it is a strategy for getting avoidants to approach you. By being slightly aloof, they will feel more comfortable being with you.

Give Up on Saving Them

You are guaranteed to experience disappointment or heartache if you enter a relationship to fix or save them. The only thing that you can hope for is that you make them feel safe enough that they desire to change themselves.

How to More Effectively Relate to an Avoidant Partner

Those who have an avoidant attachment style have a compelling need for independence and to avoid emotional intimacy. The most compatible person for such an individual is someone who is also very independent. Based on this, the following are suggestions for communicating with an avoidant partner:

Give Them Space

When your partner wants space, do your best to honor their request. Not honoring their request will only make them want to distance themselves even more so. The important thing is not to take their desire for space personally.

Acknowledge Your Differences

Learn to accept that your partner's need for connection and affection may be very different than your own. Understand that just because they do not feel the way they do does not mean that they do not love you.

Encourage Disclosure

Practice active listening when your partner discloses what they are thinking about or what they are feeling. Active listening means being supportive, nonjudgmental, and not trying problem solve. You are compassionately listening to understand what they are trying to say and to allow them to express themselves.

Develop Self-Reliance

Becoming self-reliant is the most effective way to win the trust of an avoidant partner and maintain the relationship. Develop your own interest and nurture yourself by spending time with your friends, engaging in your own interests, and taking time for self-care. By you becoming more self-reliant, your partner may become more open to taking a risk by becoming more emotionally intimate.

Let Go of Unrealistic Expectations

The more you learn about your partner's attachment style, the less likely you will take your partner's behavior personally. Having unrealistic expectations for the relationship will not serve you or your partner.

Communicate Your Needs Successfully

Having an avoidant partner does not mean suppressing how you feel or your needs. Rather, it is learning how to express your feelings and needs in a way that is assertive, clear, and open. If you come across as being emotional, needy, or demanding, it will trigger them.

Accept Your Partner Just the Way They Are

Do not try to fix your partner or try to save them. It is important to remember that your partner is behaving in response to deep-seated patterns that have existed since childhood. It is important to recognize your limitations and that no one is perfect.

Ways to Support Your Avoidant Partner

It is not uncommon for people to change their attachment styles as they grow older or through life experiences. For this reason, it is possible to enjoy a romantic relationship with an avoidant partner if both parties are willing to work on it. Of course, you cannot change them; they need to want to change. The following are suggestions for how you can support your avoidant partner.

Let Them Know Your Motivation

When you do something for your partner, let them know that you wanted to do it for them, not because you felt that they needed help. As stated earlier, avoidants do not want to accept help from others because they feel accepting help indicates weakness or neediness. Additionally, they may become concerned that they are becoming a burden to you and that it will drive you away.

Listen Without Being Judgmental or Being Defensive

Should you reach the point in your relationship when your avoidant partner starts sharing their concerns with you, be careful in the way that you respond. You will need to walk a fine line between giving them assurance that things will work out and not getting caught up in their fears.

Let Me Count the Ways

Express to your avoidant partner all the different ways that you appreciate them. You can do this throughout the day whenever you can think of something sincere to tell them. When expressing your appreciation for them, make your comments plain and simple. Though they may not reciprocate, it will help dispel any doubts that they may have about the relationship.

Make Self-Care a Priority

While providing emotional support to your avoidant partner is important, it is just as important that you care for your own emotional health. Whenever you feel that you may be too demanding of your partner or you feel that you are becoming too needy, take time to take care of yourself. While doing this is important in any relationship, it is especially important in a relationship with an avoidant personality. Consider things like spending time with friends, meditation, or exercise.

If you are truly involved with a person with an avoidant attachment style, you will have a lot of emotional work ahead of you. However, it is not an entirely different game than being in a relationship with someone with a secure attachment style. You are addressing the same areas of concern; it is just that you need to be extra mindful of the way that you do things.

CHAPTER 8

Avoidant Attachment Style and Boundaries

When you hear the word "boundaries," what comes to your mind? For many, that word brings thoughts of creating distance or building walls to protect ourselves from others. In truth, creating boundaries creates liberation, increasing the probability of enjoying a healthy and respectful relationship. More importantly, it reinforces a sense of dignity for us and others.

Instead of creating distance or building walls, boundaries create the foundation for a healthy and thriving relationship. But what are boundaries? Boundaries are rules that we create for ourselves that promote respect for each other. Setting boundaries allows us to feel comfortable in a relationship, and they build self-esteem. These three items, respect, feeling comfortable, and healthy self-esteem, are crucial for a healthy relationship.

Rather than constraining a relationship, boundaries cultivate mutual respect. They allow each person to feel comfortable in the relationship and prevent unnecessary arguments, misunderstandings, or hurt feelings. In relationships, boundaries indicate what each person's limits are.

By understanding each other's limits, we create a relationship where each person can feel respected, comfortable, and safe. Further, the boundaries that you create for yourself are flexible. As the nature of your relationship changes, you can make changes to your boundaries. In short, setting boundaries allows you to be true to who you are.

It is important to note that boundaries are needed in any relationship, regardless of how long you have been together. However, those with an insecure attachment style often have difficulties setting boundaries. In this chapter, we will explore how to implement and respond to boundaries when the avoidant attachment style is involved.

Setting Boundaries

It is never easy to say "no" to someone who you love or care about. Ironically, these are the people for which boundaries are most needed as they are the ones whom we have the most difficulty expressing limits. Boundaries provide clarity within a relationship as to what each partner expects from the other. There are two kinds of boundaries, physical and emotional.

Physical Boundaries

Physical Boundaries involve the space around us and our bodies. These boundaries include unwanted touching and the invasion of personal space. Examples of physical boundaries include:

- Not reading another person's emails or text messages.

- Not entering another person's room without permission.

- Not touching another person when it makes them uncomfortable.

Emotional Boundaries

Establishing emotional boundaries involves communicating what you need to feel safe emotionally. It also involves not letting the moods of others take priority over how you feel. You are not responsible for how others feel. It is important to learn how to respect how others feel while honoring how you feel.

It is important to know what your emotional boundaries are and to communicate them to others. The following are examples of expressing emotional boundaries:

- I appreciate that you want to find solutions to help me, but what I need is for you to just listen to me.

- I do not want to talk about it now. Can we talk about it when it is a better time?

- It is difficult for me to share with you when I feel like you dismiss my feelings.

- I can see that this is a difficult time for you; I think we need to have some space to be alone.

- When you are upset, you take it out on me, and that is not fair.

Healthy versus Unhealthy Boundaries

Healthy boundaries allow you to communicate your wants and needs while at the same time respecting the wants and needs of those around you. Examples of healthy boundaries include:

- Your ability to say "no," and honor the wishes of others when they say "no."

- You have the ability to clearly and assertively communicate your wants and needs.

- You are able to respect and honor your needs and those of others.

- You have the ability to respect the beliefs, opinions, and values of others.

- You have the ability to freely express yourself where it is appropriate.

- You are able to be flexible in your boundaries without compromising yourself.

Unhealthy boundaries result in us feeling emotionally or physically unsafe within the relationship. Examples of unhealthy boundaries include:

- You have difficulty in saying "no" or accepting "no" from others.

- You have difficulty communicating your wants and needs.

- You readily compromise your beliefs, personal values, or opinions to satisfy others.

- You are manipulative or coercive when trying to get others to do things they do not wish to do.

- You disclose too much personal information.

Why Setting Boundaries is Important

When you set boundaries for yourself, you protect yourself from being manipulated or taken advantage of. Further, you strengthen your self-esteem. Additionally, you improve the quality of your relationships because the other person knows what your expectations are. Setting boundaries also improves relationships because they provide you with a safe space to grow and become vulnerable. Relationships thrive when each person can feel safe to be who they are and express themselves, allowing them to grow and move beyond their comfort zone.

When dating, setting boundaries provides clarity in the relationship from the first day. By communicating your boundaries to the other person, they learn what you expect in a relationship. In turn, how they respond to you will let you know if you should continue to see them.

Boundaries and the Attachment Styles

Each of the attachment styles tends to respond to boundaries differently. Those with a secure attachment style tend to understand the importance of boundaries and are respectful of them. Those with an anxious attachment style tend to have more difficulty respecting boundaries and are more likely to violate their partner's need for space.

Those with an avoidant attachment style are more likely to feel that their boundaries have been violated than the other attachment styles, which makes sense because, by nature, they have a tendency to distance themselves emotionally and physically. Because they tend to suppress their emotions, they are less likely to get angry when their boundaries have been intruded upon. Also, when someone with this attachment style intrudes on the boundaries of others, their motivation for doing so is usually out of concern for the other person's well-being.

Things to Consider When Setting Boundaries

The following are suggestions for when setting boundaries with someone who has an avoidant attachment style:

Identify Your Own Need for Boundaries

Take time to reflect on what you need to feel safe, both emotionally and physically, within the relationship. One way you can do this is to think about the behavioral patterns in your current or past relationships that made you feel safe and those that did not. Identify the patterns that supported your bond with your partner. For example, if you need your partner to respect and not dismiss your concerns, that is a boundary that you need to create.

Also, when choosing your boundaries for the relationship, it is important to check in with yourself. Is the boundary something that you need to feel safe in the relationship, or is it an excuse to put up a wall between you and your partner? This can be clarified to yourself by asking yourself what the goal of your boundaries is.

Determine Your Attachment Style

Identifying your attachment style can be helpful when determining what boundaries, you need within the relationship. If you have an avoidant attachment style, you will have less of a need for proximity to your partner than if you had an avoidant attachment style.

Be Honest and Open in Your Communication

Being honest and open with someone you love can be difficult. However, it is the only way to set boundaries. It may be difficult, but not having boundaries that are clearly communicated will more likely lead to relationship issues down the line. To make it easier for you, start small and focus on one boundary at a time. Also, if communicating your boundaries to your partner makes you nervous, write them out and practice saying them in front of a mirror.

When communicating your boundaries, avoid saying "you," as it may sound accusatory. Instead, stay calm and use more "I" statements. Below are examples:

- "I feel_____ when I am spoken to that way."

- "Whenever_____ happens, I feel_____."

- "I do not appreciate the way that I am being spoken to at this moment."

- "I do want to talk to you about this, but right now, it is not the right time for me.

- "I need more time to think about it, but I will let you know."

- "I would like to help you, but right now, I have too much going on."

It is a Two-Way Street

While you have your relationship needs, your partner has their own. Further, they may not understand what those needs are, let alone how to express them to you. It is important that you and your partner learn to communicate with each other in an open and nonjudgmental way. By doing this, you will have taken a big step toward a more balanced and healthier relationship.

CHAPTER 9

Avoidant Attachment Style and the Power of Mindfulness

This book has provided a wide range of suggestions for how to cope with an avoidant attachment style. In most cases, working with a therapist will be the most effective way to learn how to manage the way the thoughts and behaviors that are associated with this attachment style.

The reason for this is that the thoughts and behaviors of this attachment style are deeply rooted within the person. Learning to overcome these tendencies involves awareness and overcoming a great deal of resistance from within ourselves. There is, however, a powerful way to assist you in creating a healthier attachment style, which is through the practice of mindfulness.

Running on Autopilot

Have you ever misplaced something, like your car keys, and were unable to find them? Perhaps, you gave up looking for them, or you got distracted by something. Either way, you returned to your normal activities. Then, sure enough, you find your keys! You find them in a place where you failed to look, or you find them out in the open. You just did not see them while searching.

Why did you not find your keys when you were searching for them? The answer to that question is simple; you were not being mindful. Here is another example. Have you ever walked into a room and forgot why you entered it? I am sure you have, as we have all done this. Why did we do this? It is the same answer; we were not being mindful.

These are just two examples of how we become caught up in thought, which keeps us from experiencing the present moment. Most of our thoughts involve the future or the past. The thoughts that we have of the past are our memories. The thoughts that we have of the future are our anticipations. Because we spend so much time caught up in the past and the future, our attention is not on what is happening in the present moment. It is for this reason that we cannot find our car keys or why we forget our reasons for entering the room.

So, what does mindfulness have to do with an avoidant attachment style or another insecure form of attachment? Those who have an avoidant attachment style are often focused on the memories of their past or their fears of what may happen in the future.

We continue to operate by the same kind of thinking that we have operated from for most of our lives. Our thoughts, feelings, and actions are recycled from the past. In other words, we are operating from autopilot. Because we are operating from past thoughts, we have the same anticipations of what will happen in the future, which is why we feel triggered.

What has just been described is true for all of us, whether we have an avoidant attachment or not. At a conscious level, we believe that we have free choice in how we will respond to a situation. While we have the capacity to do so, most of us are not operating from free choice. Rather, we are following the habitual thoughts and patterns of behavior that have guided us in the past. It is only when we extend our awareness beyond our habitual thinking that we can experience the present moment in a way that has not been tainted by the memories of our past or our anticipation of the future.

What is Mindfulness?

Mindfulness is nothing more than awareness. To be aware is to be aware of what is being experienced at the moment. The practice of mindfulness dates back 2,500 years but has not been practiced on a societal level for a long time. Only recently has mindfulness regained popularity.

Have you ever seen a magnificent sunset or other natural wonder? Do you remember what it was like to hold your child for the first time? Can you recall what it was like when you spent time being with the person who you were in love with? We have all experienced moments like these, moments where we felt fully present. We were not caught up in our thinking. During these moments, we felt alive and complete. We experienced moments of stillness where we were not caught up in our plans or worries. These are the moments where we were fully present, though perhaps just momentarily.

The Nature of Thought

Most of the time, we are not mindful. Instead of being fully present, we are caught up in our thoughts. When we get caught up in our thoughts, we cannot be present. The reason for this has to do with our relationship with our thoughts. We often personalize our thoughts, meaning that we take on their identity. If we have angry thoughts, we become angry. If we have worrisome thoughts, we become worried, and if we have loving thoughts, we become loving. When we personalize our thoughts, they become the lens through which we experience reality. This is particularly true when it comes to our beliefs.

Beliefs are thoughts about which we have a sense of certainty about. In other words, we believe them to be true. Our beliefs determine what we focus on and how we respond to a situation. If you believe that you cannot do something, you will focus on all the reasons why you cannot do it. Because of this, your response will be consistent with your beliefs. You will not give your best effort, or you may not even try.

Now, try this simple exercise:

1. Sit or lie down, close your eyes, and relax.

2. As you relax further, visualize a beautiful sunset. Visualize it with as much detail as possible. Note: Everyone visualizes, though this ability varies from person to person. Some people can see their visualizations in vivid detail, while the visualizations of others can be very vague or faint. This does not matter. Just make your visualization as real as possible according to your ability.

3. Now visualize a black cat and see it as vividly as possible.

4. Lastly, visualize a full moon. Again, make it as real as possible.

5. Now open your eyes.

During this visualization exercise, you visualized a beautiful sunset, a black cat, and a full moon. At no time did you confuse yourself with any of these visualizations? You knew that you were not the sunset, the black cat, or the full moon; you were the observer of these things. These visualizations were just thoughts that took on a visual dimension.

You did not identify with these thoughts. The reason for this is that these thoughts were not considered as being important by your mind, so you did not identify with them.

When you practice mindfulness, you will be less likely to personalize your beliefs, so you will be less likely to run on autopilot. You will be able to evaluate the situation and respond in an empowering way. The following is an example:

Greg has an avoidant attachment style. His partner is feeling frustrated and wants to talk to him about it. As Greg listens, he experiences uneasy feelings as he senses that it is going to lead to an argument. Greg's natural instincts kick in, and Greg emotionally closes down to protect himself. He then leaves the room, which leaves his partner feeling unheard.

The reason why Greg shut down was because he identified with the thoughts that he was experiencing. His thoughts and beliefs were telling him that experiencing his emotions, or the emotions of his partner, would lead to a negative outcome.

It is important to point out that we not only identify with our thoughts, but we also identify with our emotions. Our attachment styles are based on beliefs that we do not question and with which we identify. As you experienced in the previous exercise, it is possible to have thoughts and not identify with them.

If Greg practiced mindfulness, he would have an awareness of the thoughts and emotions that were arising from within him. Further, he would not judge what he was thinking or feeling. He would be accepting of their existence and allow them to present themselves without identifying with them.

Because Greg would not be identifying with his thoughts and feelings, he would be able to evaluate whether they accurately reflect what is happening in the situation with his partner.

Mindfulness Exercises

The following exercises will help you cultivate mindfulness. The more you practice these exercises, the more skillful you will become in becoming mindful. As you develop your mindfulness skills, your awareness of what you are experiencing will become more expansive.

Mindful Breathing

The following exercise will allow you to develop the ability to slow down your thoughts and increase the power of your awareness.

1. Find a place to sit down, making sure that you are comfortable. Try to find a place that offers solitude and is free of distractions. With practice, you will be able to practice in almost any kind of environment, regardless of the distractions that may exist.

2. Close your eyes and allow yourself to relax. Breathing normally, place your attention on the flow of your breath through your nose. Focus on the sensations that you experience as you inhale and exhale. Notice the sensation of your breath as you inhale. Experience the sensations of air entering your nasal cavity and your chest and abdomen rising. When exhaling, notice the sensations in your abdomen and chest falling and that of the air leaving your nasal cavity.

3. Continue to observe the flow of breath as it courses through your body. Feel yourself become more and more relaxed with each breath you take.

4. As you practice this technique, you are bound to experience your mind wandering as you get distracted by thoughts. As soon as you are aware that this has happened, gently redirect your focus back to your breath. Do not judge yourself when losing your concentration, regardless of how often this happens. The more you practice, the more you will be able to maintain your concentration without being distracted.

5. Similarly, if you experience distracting sensations or emotions, do not judge these either. Simply accept these distractions without trying to change or avoid them and continue to focus on your breath.

The goal of mindful practice is to become aware of thoughts, emotions, and sensations without getting involved with them. With continued practice, you will discover that these phenomena of the mind and body are not who you are; they are objects of the mind, and you are the one who is aware of them.

Mindfulness of the Sensations of the Body

Our body experiences innumerable sensations, yet we are so distracted in our daily lives we often are unaware of them. This mindfulness exercise will help you develop greater awareness of your body's sensations.

1. Lie down on the floor or a mat (Using your bed for this exercise is discouraged as you may fall asleep.

2. Place your attention on the movement of your breath as you inhale and exhale.

3. As you follow your breath, become aware of the sensations of your body. Do you detect a tingling in your feet or hands? Do you sense pressure or stiffness in your back, shoulders, or neck? Allow yourself to experience every sensation that you are aware of. Do not try to change them, ignore them, or judge them as being good or bad. Simply allow yourself to experience them.

4. Notice that the sensations you feel are not stable as they constantly change in their degree of intensity, while some may seem to appear, disappear, and then reappear.

5. Allow yourself to experience any given sensation for as long as you desire. When you are ready, just move on to another sensation.

6. Be sure to continue breathing as you perform this exercise.

7. Continue to practice this exercise as long as you wish.

Relaxation

Progressive relaxation is an exercise that relieves stress and promotes relaxation by sequentially tightening the body's muscles. Besides relaxing the body and developing greater awareness of the body's sensations, doing this exercise before going to bed can be helpful if you have trouble sleeping.

1. Lie down in bed and allow yourself to relax and be comfortable.

2. Focus on your breathing for a few minutes, paying attention to your breath as it travels through your body during inhalation and exhalation.

3. Close your eyes and breathe. Notice how your abdomen rises and falls as your breath flows in and out.

4. Feel the relaxation in your body as you breathe.

5. When you exhale, pay attention to the sensations in your body. Do you feel more relaxed?

6. Curl your toes. Hold it for a few seconds, and then relax. Feel the sensation of relaxation.

7. Tighten your thighs. Hold it for a few seconds, and then relax. Feel the sensation of relaxation. As you breathe out, feel your legs becoming heavier and more relaxed.

8. Tighten the muscles of the buttocks, hold them for a few seconds, and then relax. Feel the sensation of relaxation.

9. Tighten the muscles of your abdomen. Hold it for a few seconds, and then relax. Feel the sensation of relaxation.

10. Take three deep breaths using your diagram. As you inhale, focus on your abdomen rising. When exhaling, focus on your abdomen falling. After taking three deep breaths, inhale for a fourth breath and hold it. Hold your breath for as long as you can. When you exhale, focus on the sensations of the body as the air is released from your body.

11. Raise your shoulders toward your ears, raising them as high as possible. Hold it for a few seconds, and then relax. Feel the sensation of relaxation.

12. Tilt your head back as far as possible. Hold it for a few seconds, and then relax. Feel the sensation of relaxation.

13. Raise your head toward your chest. Hold it for a few seconds, and then relax. Feel the sensation of relaxation.

14. Tighten your jaw. Hold it for a few seconds, and then relax. Feel the sensation of relaxation.

15. Raise your brow as high as possible. Hold it for a few seconds, and then relax. Feel the sensation of relaxation.

16. Tighten your brow as much as possible. Hold it for a few seconds, and then relax. Feel the sensation of relaxation.

17. Take time just to relax and enjoy the sensations of your body.

Mindfulness of the Walking

Mindfulness can be practiced anywhere and at any time, as it involves being aware of what is being experienced at the moment. The following is an exercise for walking in mindfulness.

1. When first practicing this exercise, it helps to start with designating a short distance (approximately ten feet) in which you will practice mindful walking. You can extend the distance as you get more comfortable with this exercise.

2. With your route marked out, walk the distance of your route at a relaxed pace. As you walk, place your awareness on the sensation of the sole of your shoes as they contact the ground. Make sure as you are walking that you continue to breathe.

3. As you become more skillful in focusing on the sensations of walking, you can extend your awareness of what is happening in your environment. Listen to the sound of birds singing, the wind blowing, the sound of cars, or the sound of people talking. As always in mindful practice, do not judge, analyze, or evaluate anything you experience; your only job is to be aware.

Mindfulness in Eating

Have you ever eaten while watching television or talking to someone, then realized that you have consumed your meal without any memory of doing so? Perhaps you realized that you ate your meal but had no memory of really tasting it? When we eat this way, we are not mindful of our eating. As a matter of fact, many problems with digestion or maintaining our proper weight are due, in part, to not eating mindfully. When we are not eating mindfully, we deny ourselves savoring our food as our minds are elsewhere.

When practicing mindful eating, it is important to set up your environment so that you will not be distracted as you eat. You can eat alone or find someone who would be interested in eating mindfully with you, meaning there is to be no conversation while eating. Also, turn off all electronic devices and ensure you have everything you need to enjoy your meal, so you do not have to get up to get something while eating.

Lastly, it is recommended that you eat a healthy meal. As the purpose of practicing mindfulness is mental well-being, you also want to enjoy physical health.

1. Take time to relax and focus on your breath. Allow yourself to relax.

2. When you are ready, look at your food, and observe its color, shape, and texture.

3. Take in its aroma. How does your food smell? Is its aroma weak, mild, or strong?

4. Now taste your food but do so mindfully. Take only bite-size pieces and take your time before swallowing them. Allow yourself to savor its taste and how it feels in your mouth.

5. When you are ready, swallow your food.

Showering Mindfully

How many times have you taken a shower, only to realize while your body was in the shower, your mind was elsewhere? You can practice mindfulness in everything you do, and showering is no different. Taking a shower mindfully is a great way to become more in touch with your body, its sensations, and awareness of the present moment.

When taking a shower, you want your full attention on the experience of taking a shower, not on your memories or your thoughts of the future. Your only job is to take in all the sensory experiences of taking a shower. It is only natural that thoughts will arise while taking a shower, which is okay. Do not react to your thoughts; ignore them and return your attention to the sensation of taking a shower. Allow yourself to experience whatever is happening at that moment.

As you take your shower, place your focus on what you are experiencing. Here are some examples:

- Place your attention on the feelings of the water running down your body.

- Feel the sensation of the water against your skin.

- Listen to the sound of your breath.

- Listen to the sound of the water cascading downward.

- Smell the shampoo or soap that you are using.

- Feel the sensations of the soles of your feet on the shower floor.

- Feel the sensations as you work the shampoo into your hair.

- Watch as the water glides down your body.

- Watch the water as it flows down the shower drain.

- Watch the water drops splatter as they contact the shower floor.

Mindful Observing

Find a place that is comfortable for you. It can be indoors or outdoors. Sit down and allow yourself to relax. For the next 10 minutes, simply observe everything around you. Observe what you experience from within yourself (i.e., thoughts, emotions, sensations, or feelings).

Whatever it is that you notice, do not judge, evaluate, or analyze it. You are just to observe it. Feel free to go longer if you wish. Practice this each day, increasing the observation time each day. When doing this exercise, you should stay relaxed. You cannot get this exercise wrong. Even if you judge, allow yourself to experience this without judgment.

CHAPTER 10

Can Your Attachment Style Change Over Time?

Can you change your attachment style? The answer to that question appears to be "no" and "yes." The literature appears to agree that we cannot change from one style to another; however, we can alter our attachment style to become more or less secure. The following are three scenarios that illustrate how a life situation can change one's attachment style:

Scenario 1:

A child grows up in a loving and supportive home and develops a secure attachment style. Having a secure attachment style, he learns to trust others and is comfortable with emotional intimacy.

When he gets older, he starts to date. Unfortunately, he experiences a series of disappointing and unhealthy relationships. His partners have insecure attachment styles. They cheat on him, lie to him, or monitor his communications on his social media accounts and cell phones.

Repeated relationships of this kind destroy his confidence, resulting in him adopting a more insecure attachment style. He moves toward the avoidant end of the attachment style spectrum.

Scenario 2:

A woman has an anxious attachment style and is in a relationship where she always feels like she is on shaky ground. She forever fears that her partner will leave or that he is cheating on her. The relationship eventually breaks up. Tired of living this way, she gets therapy and works on herself.

Her efforts pay off, and she meets someone new. Her relationship with her new partner is more characteristic of a secure attachment style. She rarely experiences feelings of anxiousness or jealousy. When she does, she knows how to deal with it healthily.

Scenario 3:

A man has an anxious attachment style. Because of this, his relationships are characterized by the constant need for validation from his partners. He decides to go to therapy and spends a lot of time working on himself. Later, he enters a new relationship. He eventually realizes his partner has an insecure attachment style. Instead of reverting to his anxious attachment style, he interacts with his partner more securely.

Research also shows that attachments may change over time as we get older. It is theorized that as we get older, we tend to have a lower tolerance for relationships that do not meet our needs as we have less time (PsychCentral, 2022).

The Research: It Does Not Take Much!

Studies have shown that a change in attachment style can occur through positive experiences of closeness and intimacy (Jackson, 2021). One study involved 70 heterosexual couples who participated in a survey regarding their relationship. The couples were then placed into two groups. The first group engaged in activities that promoted greater intimacy and closeness.

These couples took turns answering a series of questions about themselves. The questions selected by the researchers had been proven to enhance feelings of closeness. Another activity this group got involved in was partner yoga, a form of yoga that involved holding hands or other forms of physical contact while creating poses.

The second group engaged in activities that involved answering impersonal questions and individual yoga. After completing their exercises, the participants assessed the quality of their relationships.

Those in the first group, who were identified as having an avoidant style, rated the quality of their relationship higher than they did before participating in the activities. Those who were identified as having a secure or anxious attachment style did not show any change in how they perceived their relationship. This study appears to show that activities that build intimacy may be a benefit for those with an avoidant attachment style.

What is remarkable is that there was a follow-up on the participants one month later. The increase in satisfaction that the avoidant style participants reported was still there (Jackson, 2021). The study also revealed that similar results occurred in couples engaged in spontaneous home interactions. In this study, 67 heterosexual couples in a long-term relationship were asked to keep a diary every day for three weeks. They were told to record their feelings and their partner's behavior toward them (Jackson, 2021)

The study's results found that when the romantic partners of the participants behaved positively toward them, they experienced positive emotions more frequently and negative ones less frequently. They were also happier about their relationship. Positive behaviors by the romantic partners included loving behaviors and listening to the other partner.

These findings were most evident in participants with an avoidant attachment. These studies suggest that those with an avoidant attachment style are more likely to benefit from a positive relationship than those with other insecure styles.

What is encouraging about these studies is that they show that a shift to a more secure attachment style can take place by taking action that involves little time or effort. In another study, it was found that those with an avoidant attachment style could reduce the magnitude of their negative emotions by just reflecting on positive relationship memories (Jackson, 2021).

The goal of those with an anxious attachment style should be to become more responsible for themselves. It is recommended that they engage in self-care and learn to nurture themselves. Also important is that they learn to take things slow when dating.

Those who are avoidant would do well to become more attentive to their partner's needs. It would be valuable for them to reveal their vulnerability, acknowledge their need for love, learn to receive, and set their boundaries verbally. Working on these things will cultivate a more secure and interdependent relationship.

It is important to point out that creating change for both insecure attachment styles mean facing the fear of becoming dependent on someone. This is especially true after ending a codependent relationship. However, such fears normally come from being in a codependent relationship where neither partner has a secure attachment. A healthy form of dependency leads to greater interdependence by entering a secure relationship.

The fear of becoming dependent on another can also arise when seeking therapy. In this case, it is the fear of becoming dependent on the therapist. If you experience this, you would be wise to address this fear with your therapist, as this would be a teaching moment to learn how to manage your fear.

Addressing the fear of dependency with a therapist offers the opportunity to develop the skills needed to handle such situations if they arise in the future with a partner. It is here that the paradox lies. Rather than become more dependent, quality therapy can help the individual develop a more secure attachment style, leading to greater autonomy. The greater the autonomy, the more able we will be able to become emotionally intimate with others.

Final Words

One of the most important things to understand about the avoidant attachment style is that it is not some mental illness or disorder. It is a learned way of thinking and behaving. We can think of the avoidant style and the other attachment styles as being a language. We all grew up learning a certain language. Unless we have a secure attachment style, the language we grew up with no longer serves us. We need to learn a new language to live a happier and more fulfilling life.

Using language as a metaphor for attachment styles is also valuable for my next point. Just as whom we are is not defined by the language we speak; our attachment style does not define who we are as individuals. You are not your attachment style. Rather, your attachment style shapes how you think and behave within certain moments of your relationships. I hope this book motivates you to make the necessary changes so that you may live the life you deserve.

Thank You

Before you leave, I'd just like to say, thank you so much for purchasing my book.

I spent many days and nights working on this book so I could finally put this in your hands.

So, before you leave, I'd like to ask you a small favor.

Would you please consider posting a review on the platform? Your reviews are one of the best ways to support indie authors like me, and every review counts.

Your feedback will allow me to continue writing books just like this one, so let me know if you enjoyed it and why. I read every review and I would love to hear from you.

To leave a review simply go to Amazon.com, go to "Your Orders" and then find it under "Digital Orders".